Reviews from Amazon for the first volume

I think therapists beginning to work with dissociative identity disorder, or considering doing so in the future, will benefit enormously from what is shared here. It's a tough read in places—not so much in the way of graphic details but in terms of emotional impact. If you have been through a lot of abuse (and even if you haven't) then expect to be distressed by some of the details. The writer doesn't shy away from the painful reality of her past, or the damaging effects that exist in the present, but she is able to distance herself enough emotionally in some of the later sections to be able to interpret much of her own experience in order to provide psychological insight. It's not really a book which is about what happened, or how, but about the effect of it all, and how she unravelled the hidden parts of the past, and the hidden parts of herself, and somehow found within herself the drive to recovery. I can't think of another person writing autobiographically within this field who writes in this way, but understanding the connections (and disconnections) within herself/her parts was something I found very helpful in understanding DID. It is a difficult balance between describing trauma—and the traumatic and conflicting emotions—and reflecting on healing and recovery. To write like she does, and in the way she does, gives hope both to people surviving abuse of any kind and to those who support survivors of abuse.

By Anonymous

This is a very real, honest and thought-provoking read. As a sufferer of DID myself, the affirmation that I am not alone and other people have the same things to deal with is hugely relieving. This book covers some of the hardest topics to explain with clarity and plain talking, such as shame, guilt and denial. This book however also covers topics deeply personal to the author. These are covered without sensationalism and emphasise the fact that this is a disorder that is caused, not just occurring. The book has a bit of 'science' in there too providing some clear explanations for those suffering with or dealing with someone with DID. I rate the book 5 stars.

By Sarah Power

Carolyn's honest, brave, intelligent and poetically written essays about living with and recovering from DID are a real gift. I read it from cover to cover, and then began all over again.

By Elizabeth

Very positive, informative and courageous book. I was moved to tears. The most important message: recovery is the best revenge.

By Eve

i

Carolyn's style of writing imparts an incredible depth of information without being textbook-like, and also shares the human side of her personal journey without sensationalising the trauma or DID. It helpfully spans the pervasive divide between 'survivor books' and 'therapist books'. It doesn't unnecessarily focus on the abuse itself, but more on the legacy of that trauma in our thinking, feeling, bodies, and ways of relating to others and ourselves—recognising that 'symptoms' are often very logical adaptive responses to the trauma which isn't seen by those around us now. And it appears for Carolyn as well as the reader, that hopes comes from acknowledging what happened, gaining understanding and insight into its effects but then from this finding ways to make things different now. Thankfully she doesn't glibly recommend any 1-2-3 magical steps to doing this, but clearly conveys that recovery in an ongoing process that requires a lot of good therapy and a lot of hard work! She writes in a way that through countless 'How did she know that's what's in my head?!' moments enables the reader (be it a survivor, therapist or anyone else) to feel less alone and less 'mad or bad' and therefore far more hopeful. I would recommend this book for everyone.

By K

This book, as others have said, is excellent for those wishing to understand more about DID and to read from the point of view of someone who experiences it. It is also, though, a book about trauma and surviving and the pure logic of the systems which may look illogical to those who have not suffered trauma. If I used the word must, I would call it a must-read for all working in Mental Health. We need to know these things exist and how our beings cope with them.

By Minnehaha

This book is a quick read, but definitely a worthwhile read. For anyone who struggle with a dissociative disorder at all, and struggles with getting people to understand what you're trying to talk about when you try to explain your experiences, then this book is great. When reading this book I felt like I was reading someone explain what I struggled to put into words put into words perfectly. This book alone made me feel less like a freak, less alone, and less self-doubting of, 'Could this experience really be real?' because some healthcare professionals are very sceptical, and overall unhelpful when I've tried to talk about these experiences. But finally, finally I found someone who could explain it, relate to me, and really show me that life can go on with a dissociative disorder.

By Monica Smith

A very insightful and informative book. Helpful for both survivors, families and professionals. For those working in a counselling or therapeutic capacity, this is a must-read. Thank you for being so honest and real.

Claire Lockwood

As someone who is also living with DID, I found this book to be the most helpful and inspirational book I have ever read. So well written and I would recommend this book to anyone who is living with dissociation, dealing with trauma and the repercussions of childhood abuse. I would also recommend this book to professionals working in this field.

By N & Co

I am a counsellor working with women with complex needs and this book gave me a whole new insight into DID and the effect it can have on an individual. A thoroughly honest and personal diary which moved me to tears. Thank you to Carolyn for sharing her story. I would recommend this to anyone working with clients who have DID or who are dealing with childhood trauma.

By AB

Would recommend anyone who has been abused to read this book. It has actually started to help me change my mindset and given me an invaluable insight into the lifelong effects of child abuse (sexual). I have started to open up and am now on a quest to heal as much as I can. THANK YOU for this book, Carolyn. It has been a key for me. Brilliant!

By Kathleen Douglas

This is an amazing account and glimpse into the world of someone who suffers with DID as a result of extreme childhood trauma and the recovery process. Excellently written, poignant, challenging at times. Wonderful insight into the therapeutic process from the client perspective. I have gained so much from reading this. Highly recommended.

By Jeannie D

Carolyn Spring's writing is really beautiful and descriptive. Although this is not an easy book to read, it would help people to understand the perspective of a person experiencing the symptoms of dissociative identity disorder.

L Everett

Very well written and from the heart. Carolyn shows such strength and determination. A down-to-earth description of what it's like to be an abuse survivor — recovery is possible, so never give up hope.

By Meaghan Ebbage-Taylor

Very interesting book and very interesting to hear from this perspective. I heard Carolyn present and she was very articulate and interesting.

By Jayne Mcconkey

An inspirational piece of writing, which is extremely powerful, as well as being insightful and informative. I would definitely recommend this to both therapists and survivors.

By Neb

A really great book that I couldn't put down! I would definitely recommend this to everyone interested in FACTS, not fiction... the author writes beautifully from the heart.

By ellenp79

Carolyn beautifully articulated what I've felt but never been able to say. Great read for abuse survivors and therapists.

By Maureen Blackabee

An excellent book, very understandable. Would recommend it to survivors and therapists alike.

By Amazon Customer

A courageous book that needed to be written about this complex and disturbing condition of dissociative identity disorder.

By Avid Reader

The person I gave this to said that it was the first time he had read something that explained the things he felt and experienced every day after a childhood of trauma. He said his trauma was not as bad as some people's but he could relate to how it affects adult life and social interactions after reading this book. I am so glad that it and I could help him.

By Erin B

I have just been assessed by a psychotherapist who says I have DID, so I have been trawling the internet for information and came across this book. It contains all the information I have been looking for and is also an incredibly useful resource for close friends and partners who are also trying to understand.

By George

Excellent book, especially for other survivors with as yet an unidentified diagnosis of the mental and physical health conditions they suffer from as a consequence of their abuse... as was the case with my own daughter (now an adult).

By Christina Valentine

Essential read for partners and close friends and family of people with DID. Indicates first steps and what to expect in early therapy from the view of the person receiving therapy. Excellent read, brave author. Thank you.

By Anke Smith

As someone who is just starting recovery from dissociation, this has been a very helpful and insightful read. Difficult at times but certainly something I will read again. Thank you Carolyn for putting this together.

By Pen Name

This is an amazing book and I am grateful that Carolyn had the courage to write about her experiences. Her book also gives helpful information about recovery from trauma.

By Linda Hoyle

Brilliant insight into deep personal issues faced by the author. Very helpful to anyone in similar situations or professional counsellors and psychotherapists.

By Lorna

Excellent book. My heart goes out to Carolyn and what she's been through. I'm a counselling student and found this book hugely beneficial to my studies.

By Amandabo

I like the way this author draws on personal experience. It is brilliantly written and tis true—recovery is the best revenge!

By Mrs Parsley

For anyone who has an interest in DID this should be required reading as it's both inspirational and informative.

By Ange

Everyone in the medical profession should read this, then they might actually believe in DID!

By Babyduck

recovery
is my best revenge

recovery

is my best revenge

collected essays volumes 1 & 2

by CAROLYN SPRING

CSP
carolyn spring publishing

Recovery is my Best Revenge

Published by Carolyn Spring
Publishing (Huntingdon, UK)

3 Archers Court, Huntingdon, PE29 6XG, UK

www.carolynspring.co.uk

© 2016 Carolyn Spring

First edition
Volume One first published as an e-book in 2014

ISBN: 978-0-9929619-3-0

TO SIMON & JULIA

You have made this book possible
through your love, faith, kindness,
compassion and friendship.
Even Charlie helped.
Thank you.

ABOUT THE AUTHOR

Carolyn Spring

Carolyn Spring is an author and publisher as well as being Director of PODS (Positive Outcomes for Dissociative Survivors) and its charity framework START (Survivors Trauma and Abuse Recovery Trust). PODS works to make recovery from dissociative disorders a reality through training, informing and supporting, and Carolyn delivers all the PODS training as well as editing the magazine/journal *Multiple Parts* which is produced three times a year. She developed dissociative identity disorder (DID) as a result of prolonged and extreme childhood abuse but believes passionately in recovery and the dignity and respect that is due to all human beings.

For further information please go to:
www.carolynspring.co.uk
www.pods-online.org.uk
www.start-online.org.uk.

CONTENTS

Volume One

Recovery from what?

T he sunshine is leaking through the blinds. I stand up to tilt them further, to erase the shaft of light from the top of my computer screen. And that's when I see it. It is raining leaves. The great, grand horse chestnut trees that block out the sky from my office window are shedding their skin and, in the haze of an autumn morning, the air is raining leaves. It is sad, and beautiful, and sore. It is death. A part of this tree is dying. In the summer it was vivid with the glare of green, those splayed-out fingers of leaves swaying and shimmering and rustling in the wind. Now they are dying, and the ground below is ankle deep with gnarled, brown fingernails.

It happens every year and yet I have never been caught up in it as I am for this one moment. Because suddenly I see it. The great tree is breaking down. Its summer beauty is gone. It is a ragged, pathetic stump. Much like I was, when I broke down too.

I carried, unknowing within me, compacted layers of unremembered trauma. My life worked to a level. I was 'normal,' even successful. But unremitting bouts of pain and chronic fatigue were ever with me, and belied my normality. I couldn't fathom the cause of my illnesses. I couldn't comprehend the source of my dread, a terror that gnawed at my guts deep within me and yet seemed to have neither beginning nor end. In shame, I hid my defects as best I could and smiled defiantly at a world that I was determined, and yet unable, to conquer.

And then in 2005 I started to shed my leaves. I had a 'breakdown' and was stripped of all pretence of strength or competence or sanity. And that unremembered trauma returned—as it felt at the time—to devour me.

I was overwhelmed, and dysfunctioning, for a good many years. I didn't understand it. I couldn't control it. It was shameful. It was costly. Several times, I nearly killed myself. Many more times I self-harmed. The painful unrememberings began to flood back through my bones, seeping into my joints with unexplained pain and unremitting distress. They worked up through my muscles and entered my mind. I began to remember. Viscous memories suffocated me. It was for good reason that I had put them out of mind for so long.

That morning, watching the leaves rain through the sky, I suddenly realised that the tree was not dying. And I was not dying either. The tree must shed its leaves, to protect itself from winter. It sheds them in order to prepare for new growth. The dying leaves are a ritual of death to prepare for the ritual of life. And the same was happening with me. I was dying in order to bloom.

In the midst of flashbacks and nightmares, it didn't feel much like new life. The dying was painful. Many times I was tempted to hack the useless tree to a stump. I couldn't see ahead to the next spring. I couldn't imagine new life. I was the leaves tossed away by the branches, decaying and rotting and swirling around with litter on the ground. I felt dead. And so I felt that I deserved only to die.

It took a long time to figure out what was 'wrong' with me. I eventually learned that there is nothing wrong with a tree for shedding its leaves, and there was nothing wrong with me for what I was experiencing. I had survived trauma by blocking it out. The technical term was 'dissociation.' This shedding, now, this breakdown, was the trauma trying to heal. I was 32, and for perhaps the first time my mind knew that it was safe to begin this recovery slog. The mind always knows when the right time is.

It didn't seem the right time to me. But never would have seemed the right time to me. I had survived by dissociating, and would have continued to do so, if my mind had not been determined to heal. Something deep within me wanted a life that was abundant, not simply to survive. I wanted to know truth in my innermost parts, not hide in the shadows within myself. A primal instinct for life won out over the survival tactics of avoidance and denial.

Eventually I landed with the diagnosis of dissociative identity disorder. It explained so much but it was hard to accept. It was a strange new identity. For a year I had been switching uncontrollably, unpredictably, into other parts of my personality. My shame ran so deep that my mind chose not to remember. So I was amnesic not just for my past trauma, but for the past five minutes, the past five hours— any time when other parts of me were 'out.' My husband witnessed me 'going mad' but at last with the label we both began to understand that there was nothing insane in the way I was reacting. It was supremely logical in the light of my childhood. Parts of me were stuck back there, in the rapes, in the torture, so when they crawled under the table and whispered, 'We don't want the nasty men to come,' there was nothing crazy about it. It was a very real memory, being relived in the here-and-now.

Nine years on, I've remembered 'the nasty men,' and the 'nasty women' too. I've remembered a lot. Much of it is sketchy, more the surge and fall of emotion than the steadiness of thought. And I have been recovering. Much of that recovery has been facilitated through therapy. Much of it has been contained and knit together by my then husband. And much of it has been gained through reading and understanding. I began to learn about DID and to see it as a creative survival mechanism for surviving otherwise unendurable trauma. I began to see that the traumatised 'child' parts of myself were in conflict with the apparently normal 'adult' parts of me. The former were stuck in the trauma, reliving it as if it were still ongoing and therefore unable to process and metabolise it, whereas the latter were convinced that avoidance would win the day.

The work of recovery has been to resolve those conflicts and start to live as an integrated person who can both operate successfully as an adult whilst accepting and soothing the traumas of childhood. I believe in hope for recovery. And I have grave doubts about the medical model that attempts to heal me with drugs to 'rebalance' chemicals in my brain. I have learned that there is nothing wrong with my brain. It has adapted to cope with uncopeable circumstances, and it's adapting now to a new life that is safe and free from trauma. My brain, my mind, my body, my mindbody—all of these integrated aspects of myself are prewired for survival. They know how to live. They know how to recover. I've just had to get out of the way and stop preventing it from happening.

Recovery is possible, because after the winter there is always the spring.

These essays are part of a wider collection of writing that I have been engaged in over the last few years. In forging my own pathway towards recovery, I have also been trying to make straight some paths for others. In 2009 I set up PODS—Positive Outcomes for Dissociative Survivors. It is now a leading organisation in the field of trauma, abuse and dissociation in the UK. Of the many things it does, producing a magazine/journal, *Multiple Parts*, has perhaps been closest to my heart. DID, and the trauma that causes it, can make you feel terribly, unbearably alone. It has been revolutionary for me to read about the experiences of other people with DID, and realise that I am not alone, and I am not unique. Through *Multiple Parts* I've also been able to share my story, and I have tried to educate and equip not just DID survivors themselves but the extensive band of everyday counsellors who come across us in clinical practice.

Those of us with DID don't tend to present ourselves in therapy with a label. Few of us understand that we even have DID. We present with a polysymptomatic salad bowl of all kinds of issues and difficulties, and only when we're safe enough do we tend to reveal the hidden parts of ourselves. The toughest battle is not in admitting these parts to the therapist, but to ourselves, and so much of the work of therapy is to build bridges between these dissociated and alienated islands of experience within ourselves. We recover when we accept and embrace who we are, and we discover what it is to be safe. We recover when we recognise that the powerlessness of trauma is just a feeling, just a memory from the there-and-then, and that we are no longer powerless in the here-and-now.

But there is little or no training about dissociative disorders in the syllabi of most counselling, psychology or psychiatry courses. So most mental health professionals haven't heard of it, and even fewer are equipped to diagnose and treat it effectively. PODS, along with a number of other pioneering organisations in this field, are working to raise awareness and make treatment for DID more readily available. For more information both about DID and the work of PODS, please go to www.pods-online.org.uk.

In the meantime, my story is beginning to be told. There is no orderly narrative in this volume of my collected essays, because life with DID isn't like that. Each chapter brings its own focus and its own particular insights. Each comes with the subtle under-voice of a different part of my personality, of the multitudes that make up the whole that is me. You can read the chapters in any order. But please do read them all.

CHAPTER ONE

Memories of Mummy

I ask, tentative, coy, and I search carefully for a reciprocal gaze and an encounter with good mummy. Blankness. All I have, in this gaze, returns blankly to me. Can I?—an anything, a *can I tell you about school today? or can I play out?* or (intruded anger) *can I be?*—and the hesitancy of me is unechoed back and I can *not*. There is no answer, no flicker of interaction. Then stuck, a moment of paralysed indecision in the ignoredness of me, and I step back just one step just one step just *one step* (I promise myself) into my inside-fog and there disappear, to a place and a *me* where it doesn't matter.

Mummy explains that we must brush our teeth. The bigness of adulthood around me and a towering pedestal basin. We must brush our teeth because little men live in our mouth with hammers and they hammer away at our teeth all the time and if we don't brush them away then we won't have any teeth left. *But then we can grow some more.* No you can't, once your adult ones come, that's it. *That's it?* I feel cheated. I read somewhere that whales or sharks or something get lots and lots of teeth and it's not fair if I don't. I feel cheated and wrong. This is new to me and it doesn't—*doesn't*—fit. There is something inescapable about my doom. *And I really don't like having little men in my mouth.*

Somebody said something about the potatoes being burnt or the carrots being undercooked and the gravy was spilled on the table and then *ERUPTION!* and terror of Mummy *crying*, flailing in angry crying spurting shouting raging shrieking wail... and gone. *I shouldn't have spilled the gravy.* Tummy-dissolving terror and the nausea of dread of terrible things, things that shouldn't be, humming just humming around behind my eyes and I can't see, I can't see, but I know. Mummy has gone to her bedroom and I edge in, bravely, cowardly, *I'm sorry, Mummy, I'm sorry, Mummy.* Then sobs and bitterness and spite and 'No one appreciates me' and *I do, Mummy, I do, Mummy, thank you, Mummy, thank you, Mummy, please come back down, Mummy.* There is something awful to avert and I strain with everything *I am not* to placate and restore back to life the competent Mummy that is good and cooks Sunday lunch without complaint, the good Mummy who sits next to me opposite *him* and whose silence at mealtimes validates my own.

There is a telephone, cream, bulbous, ugly and threatening, and there is Mummy, with her hand on the handset and rage in her eyes, and there is me, little girl, *bad little girl,* silent now with hiccupy sobs and a bundle of confusion. *I don't know what the answer is.* Questions, questions, about things that I've done, *but I haven't done them, I haven't done them,* bad little girl lying, *I can't remember, I'll say I did if it makes it better,* but you're lying, you're lying, naughty girl off to the children's home, *please Mummy don't make me go, I AM sorry, I AM sorry.* So tell me *but I can't.* I could explode with the impossibility of my badness and the blankness in my head that doesn't know the answer to the questions but I will do anything, *anything,* for her to put the phone back down again. Heaving chestpained sobs and I dissolve away and the rage steps aside from me and blank compliance and *unnaughtiness* takes its place. My body trembles with the goneaway rage and I take the punishment and the phone is replaced and an orgasmic relief that I can stay, I can stay, I can stay here with good Mummy and good Daddy and sister, and him even *him.*

We stood on a bridge after playgroup and underneath on the canal a barge went by and we watched and we watched and we stood for a little while, only a little while, a little while of eternal joy of Mummy and me, watching the barge go by. We didn't go straight home; we stayed and we watched a little while on the bridge. *I love my Mummy, love my Mummy, love my good Mummy so much.*

I don't know where I was and I don't know what I'd done. I don't know who I was and I don't know where good Mummy had gone, but Mummy *now*—needles. My fingers, stretched out in white translucence, the clarity of perfect little fingernails, *needles*. In my head, a shifting, like slides going through a cine projector, and from afar I see the cold fury of a trembling Mummy hurting me, hurting me, needles up my fingernails, *hurting me*. My wrist wants to tear away from the omnipotent grasp around it, but my wrist—disconnected, not me, and compliant all at the same time. It wants to be still and submit and wait and be good. *Naughty girl, don't ever say that.* Words, words, words that have leaked from my mind onto my lips and betrayed me and now the thought-curdling pain of *pain somewhere in me* and *Be quiet!* and *I will, I will, I will, I will.* Words, words: now just a numbness of faraway, numb fingers, numb mind, numb me. *Where's Mummy gone? I want my Mummy. I want my good Mummy.*

I can't find her eyes. I talk above all the din of the coffee shop around us; she moves her shopping bags for another customer to get by; I talk and talk and hop around on the stillpond surface of events and happenings and people and things: *adult-me stuff.* I can't find her eyes. A pot of tea, a decaff cappuchinno later, and still her eyes, watery, thin, iced with the temerity of *not-knowledge* when she looks towards me: I can't find her eyes. I can't find me, her daughter, *me*.

Somewhere there is pain and *Mummy mustn't see.* I have to be good now and not show Mummy. Sometimes there's a plaster but a plaster won't stick there and *Mummy mustn't see.* I don't want Mummy to be cross, to tease me, to mock me. I will sit quietly while she's ironing and sit still in that closeness and be the good girl that she loves. There is sport on the telly and Mummy withers it with words, but words that aren't aimed at *me*; throbs and aches and sickshaky in my tummy, but while there is sport and ironing I am safe and unseen, with my good Mummy who irons so beautifully, and I wonder if I will ever iron so well one day.

She is starched and uptight like a puppet on too-taut strings. She is my mother at my wedding. Something—*someone?*—screams silently inside with the not-knowing of discomfort of posing for photographs. I want to get away, get away, get away. Where are her eyes?—and her proud civility, the Mercedes and lipstick and fifteen denier tights, all welcoming *her* guests, an arrayed spectacle of the utterly respectable. *Of course.* I crave good Mummy's smile but it wasn't her who helped me dress that morning. Thank you, thank you, thank you for everything; thank you, thank you, for the respectable spectacle of grimacing politeness and I want to get away from the contamination of shame of *this is my mother* and I don't know why. But *thank you, thank you.*

I clamber up high, so high, onto a breakfast stool in winter dusk and I read aloud to Mummy. Words, words, words on a page — words that become worlds in my mind and I finger the ochre in the picture with a wonder for far-off seaside sands. The words with which my lips struggle tumble through my mind and became the *elsewhere* of my survival. I stutter and *good Mummy* helps me with the words. *Good Mummy* helps me.

It is dark, and thick velvety curtains hang blackly in a room somewhere. I yawn and tiredness prickles my eyes while fear stiffens my back. I need a wee. I don't want to watch but it's *eyes open* or it will hurt. *Your turn next.* Mummy's lumpy, puffy body, her white back towards me, twisting on her side, raised moles on her back and hip, she's naked, *naked*. Then a man, I can't see (I won't see) and Mummy moving. I know it's Mummy because of her moles. *Where's good Mummy gone?* I don't want to watch and I am empty with the bewilderment of *Mummy and me.*

CHAPTER 2

Not mad, not bad — just traumatised

I spend a lot of time thinking that I'm 'mad.' And so do a lot of people I know. The funny thing, of course, is that for the most part none of us have adequately defined what exactly this 'madness' thing is supposed to be. It's a concept that has leaked down into grubby little recesses of our cultural psyche from disparate sources: headlines in the Daily Mail ('Blair: I kept quiet about God so I wouldn't be seen as a nutter'), comic books with their sociopathic comedy villains (The Joker, Lex Luthor), literary fantasy (The Mad Hatter) and an unsavoury social history of the 'lunatic asylum' and 'mental wards.'

It's just so normal to talk about insanity and madness. Look at the language of everyday life:
- 'I'm going to New York on holiday. How mad is that?!'
- 'He's crazy about you.'
- 'This total lunatic got on the bus without a ticket and refused to pay.'
- 'You're having another child? You must be mad!'
- 'My boss is a psycho.'
- 'Those nutters in the Government just don't get the impact their policies are having.'
- 'The English language is insane.'
- 'I'm as mad as a hatter.'
- 'You've totally lost the plot.'
- 'He's one stick short of a bundle.'

- 'If you keep acting like that, the men in white coats will come and take you away!'
- 'She's a total fruitcake.'
- 'I'm a bit OCD about housework.'
- 'I've gone a bit loopy.'
- 'You're cuckoo.'
- 'He was driving like a maniac.'
- 'My mother has got a screw loose.'
- 'It's crazy weather today.'
- 'You want to work overtime?! What are you, demented?!'
- 'That teacher is off her rocker.'
- 'Are you out of your mind?!'
- 'She was hysterically upset.'
- 'He's a bit unbalanced.'
- 'The kids were driving me mad.'

This kind of language is so common that the concepts it evokes slip under the radar of rational consideration and just hang blithely in our cultural mindspace. Of course there is such a thing as madness, lunacy, insanity! And it's something apparently so abnormal that we can joke about being 'a bit mad' knowing full well that no one will think that we're being serious. Truly 'mad' people are all locked up in mental hospitals, aren't they?

A few years ago PODS sent out a mailshot about our DID training courses. One therapist responded with an email brimming with vitriol. 'This is absolutely appalling,' she said. 'You shouldn't be running these courses. People with serious psychiatric conditions such as dissociative identity disorder should be treated as inpatients in a psychiatric hospital, not by therapists in private practice.'

Well, that's a shame, I thought. Because I don't really want to leave my home and family, my work, my friendships, my local community, and go and sit in a psychiatric unit while I get 'treated.' I don't want to be deprived of my liberty and deemed incapable of managing my own affairs. I want to keep pursuing 'recovery' with my once-a-week private therapy, because it's working.

Thank goodness this particular person is the only therapist to have responded in this way. Thank goodness people like me aren't banished to some psychiatric inpatient setting out of sight of society where our supposed 'insanity'—that would justify depriving us of our freedom and our autonomy—isn't allowed to impinge on society's consciousness. Thank goodness I'm free to contribute to society, live in my own home, and my mind is drug-free enough to be able to write these words.

The thing is, I do have what some people call a 'serious psychiatric diagnosis' (and the whys and wherefores of diagnosis I dissect elsewhere) but I'm not mad. My husband regularly said that I was one of the most sane people he had ever met. My behaviours, my feelings, my thoughts, even my beliefs might not conform to those of the majority of people in the UK but they are all entirely and utterly logical. (By the way, if 10% of the population admits to hearing voices, then is even that most quintessential of symptoms of 'madness' quite so abnormal really?) I behave, feel, think and believe the way I do for the most part because of the experiences I have had in life to date. And that's just the same for everyone else: psychiatric inpatients, therapists, teachers, politicians, cleaners and probably even mass murderers. We all respond to the world and build our interpretative mental maps of it based on our experience of it and the people in it. It's called—scientific term alert—'learning.'

The only thing insane about my life is the experiences I've had. As Jacqui Dillon from the Hearing Voices Network says, 'Bad things happen to us and they can drive us crazy.' And in an act of blatant revolutionism, Jacqui didn't even have to get a PhD to write that sentence. What seems so obvious to supposedly 'insane' people like me (people with psychiatric labels) is apparently almost unfathomable and maybe even a little psychotic to many people with letters after their name. I mean, if you're going to call 'feeling upset' something technical like 'dysphoria,' you're probably going to have to study for a great many years in academic institutions which create and then speak that language. One of my particular pet hates is the use of 'academese,' the kind of words and phrases based on Latin and Greek that only 'specialists' can understand. It's no different from Catholic priests in the Middle Ages reading only a Latin version of the Bible so that their congregants couldn't understand it and couldn't challenge their power and hegemony (and abuse). Technicalising 'sadness' and calling it 'flat affect' just obscures the meaning to segregate it from normal human experience. And it has the effect of making those of us who feel sad a lot believe that there is something intrinsically wrong with us, or that we have contracted some form of emotional 'disease' while 'scientists' (the people who are always right) prod us and poke us with their diagnostic criteria. How different it might be if the fabled 'men in white coats' actually asked us what was making us sad and cried with us about it, rather than just stigmatising us with their academic better-than-thou terminology. But that's for another day...

I had experiences throughout childhood of disorganised attachment and extreme trauma including child sexual abuse and torture. And all within a 'standard middle-class upbringing' where what happened on a night wasn't alluded to during the day, where denial was my staple diet and where I was presented with 'black' and told that it was 'white.' Despite all of that, my mind insisted on trying to reconcile these contradictions and never gave up the attempt to figure out what was really 'true.' If my mind had just accepted that 'this is the way it is,' that I really do deserve all this inhumane cruelty, that people who can be kind to you during the day can rape you at night, then I would be either dead by now or truly 'mad.' But my mind has for nearly forty years insisted on navigating a healing path through this mishmash of paradox. In doing so, it's had to exclude the 'black' so that it can focus just on the 'white' and survive a little longer. It's had to exclude the cruelty so that it can focus on the kindness. It's had to keep out of sight and out of mind many of the irreconcilable contradictions that daily life unfolded upon me. And that's a large part of what dissociation is—keeping the 'white' separate from the 'black,' the 'good mummy' separate from the 'bad mummy.' It's the definitive sign, I think, of sanity in an insane world.

Ultimately, the greatest hope we have is that our minds do in fact want to reconcile the paradoxes and understand what went on. They want to figure out how the someone who ensures that you have smart, clean uniform for school can also allow you to be taken out to be raped by groups of adults. How does the mind reconcile that? With the flexibility of a mind-in-progress, dissociation, splitting off, amnesia, is an obvious solution. Children just accept things the way they are. That's one of the reasons, I believe, why many of us seemed so 'normal' at school. We were doing a form of mental gymnastics to twist into impossible shapes, and we could, because we were children, and that was how we survived. It's when adulthood arrives with its need to form our own sense of self, of what we believe and who we are, of what behaviour is right and normal, and there is no one around to tell us what to do, that the frameworks that we existed on during childhood break down. And we call it just that: a 'breakdown.'

For me in my early thirties, I was trying to figure out who I was and what I wanted in life. I was trying to learn how to parent and build a career, trying to negotiate and construct an adult-to-adult relationship with my parents, trying to find somewhere to belong in this grown-up world that doesn't give you after-school clubs and sports teams and the daily opportunity to make and break friends in an endless supply of peers. Adult life doesn't so easily spell out to you the rules for what you need to do and when to do it by, and dictate your dress code, and organise your timetable and give you merit cards and detentions. You have to start figuring all that out for yourself. And with all the inherent, unknown contradictions in my mind of the mental maps that I had laid down up to that point in life, none of it made sense. It was at that point that the 'logic' of the world that I had lived in once and for all exploded and shattered around me and I 'went mad.'

But this 'going mad' wasn't any form of insanity at all, no matter what diagnostic manuals may tell me. This 'going mad' was my mind beginning to make its own sense of the world for the first time, for itself, and lay out all the contradictions of the insanity of my childhood for me to unpick and comprehend. I could only do that by allowing myself, for the first time, to think and to remember. It was like a process of bringing out all the complicated bits of the jigsaw that just didn't seem to fit into the picture at all and that I'd kept hidden away in the box because I couldn't face the overwhelming sense of confusion that they evoked.

But, problematically, that act of allowing out the memories, the dissociative parts of the self that I had kept firmly in the box, brought with it a collapse of my previous coping strategies and my previous 'logic' for life. Things don't work the way they used to. Life previously functioned a certain way, and then overnight, everything changes, and nothing is the same. As an analogy, a woman in her fifties goes to work in the morning and comes home in the evening and finds her husband dead in the lounge. Her life has unexpectedly been turned upside down. Suddenly, she can't do what she was going to do that evening. She can't make dinner and talk about her day and ask him to take the bin out and feed the cat. She can't just get up the next morning and go to work and pop to Tesco's on the way home and send a birthday card to her cousin. Suddenly everything is different. It's a new situation. She's got a funeral to organise, and she's never done it before, and it's overwhelming. She's used to talking about her day with her husband and he's not there. When she's upset, she's used to going to him for comfort and support, but at the point at which she most needs comfort and support, he's not there. She's not a married woman anymore; she's a widow: it's a change of identity. Her finances are different. She has to learn about the servicing schedule for the car and get someone to help her hump the Christmas tree down from the loft. Life is suddenly very, very different.

And when she goes a bit 'crazy,' when she starts crying and can't stop, when she sits and stares into space for an hour because she can't figure out what to do next or how to do it, when she doesn't want to go for a drink after work with her colleagues and can't bear their jollity, when she can't concentrate at work or remember what it was that she was doing, when she lies awake at night worrying about how to pay the mortgage... when all these things happen, no one actually says that she's gone mad. Everyone understands that she's in grief and that it will take time, perhaps a long time if the death was sudden and unexpected, for her to rearrange her life again so that the new normal becomes automatic and comfortable and comprehensible. And even then, for decades afterwards she may contend with the *why?* questions of sudden tragedy and life not being as sugar-sweet as the John Lewis adverts suggest.

But when we have a 'breakdown,' when our dissociative coping strategy that has kept our trauma or abuse at bay for years or years suddenly collapses in the lounge and dies on the floor, and we find when we come home from work that it's not there anymore, people don't see our resultant behaviour as normal. Even we ourselves think we have just 'gone mad.' We don't have a paradigm for it. And because there's no corpse in the lounge, no funeral cortège, no life insurance pay-out and a bank statement in a single name, because it's all intrapsychic and hidden in the undergrowth of our mind, then our outward behaviours do seem 'crazy.' When we can't go to work the next day, and we can't concentrate, and we keep bursting into tears, and we can't bear to socialise, and we lie awake at night, and everything seems too much, then we don't think, 'This is normal.' We think, 'I'm insane.'

Many people in an emerging 'Critical Psychiatry Network' of professionals are arguing for the 'demedicalisation of misery' and it's the most sane thing I've heard people say in a long time. When bad stuff happens to us, it's distressing. When lots of bad stuff happens to us, in ways that we simply can't cope with because it's too awful and we're too young and we don't have the support, it's distressing beyond belief. The result of that distress is what has been termed 'symptoms' of 'mental illness.' But that's suggesting that something has gone wrong in the brain. Is the widow—crying over her dead husband's belongings as she packs them away—insane? Has something gone wrong in her brain? Or is she just naturally expressing the grief and the upset and the distress that losing someone you've loved for over 30 years will naturally bring? Does she have a mental disorder?

No. And neither, I would argue, do we as trauma survivors. Should the widow be put on medication to numb down her feelings of grief and loss or should she be allowed to cry? Should friends and family gather around her and support her and be with her, help her with those boxes from the loft, take her car to the garage until she knows what a cambelt is, be with her on long, lonely evenings, send her flowers, phone her up? Or should they just tell her to go to the GP and get some 'anti-depressants' for her 'mental health problem?'

It's funny how, as a society, we feel that certain types of distress are normal and on the whole we can cope with them and tolerate them—although some people would still rather cross the road than have to talk to the recently bereaved. But when it comes to extreme trauma, when it comes to decades of abuse, criminal acts perpetrated on defenceless children which have never been prosecuted or even voiced, then we are expected to either take tablets, live in a hospital, or just get over it. The unhealed suffering, in all its technicoloured distress, is bad enough, but then to add to it, society as a whole dumps on us the stigma and rejection of a label of being 'mad.' It suggests that there's no reason for our grief and our distress, and that we have a 'disorder.'

Certainly, a lot of the so-called 'symptoms' of mental distress don't appear logical. When in my early thirties I would crawl under a table, shaking and crying and trembling, and wail, 'I don't want the nasty men to come' in a child-like voice, it didn't seem 'normal,' or 'sane,' or 'understandable'. My mind evidently couldn't cope with that contradiction either—the professional, competent me and this quivering, terrorised child-me—and so my adult brain wouldn't remember that this was what I had just done. So then my husband is faced with two apparent forms of insanity: me under the table as a child-part-of-me, then me denying that that's what I'd just done. I can and do understand why he thought I'd gone mad. It's logical only when you know the history. And you only know the history if it's allowed to be told.

For me the stigma of 'madness' caused a swell of suffering on top of my already stressed-out and distressed-out state of mind. People don't like 'mad' people. People think that 'mad' people are dangerous. If you're mad, they take your children away. If you're mad, you get locked up in a mental ward and drugged. If you're mad, no one takes you seriously or listens to what you want any more. If you're mad, no one believes what you say, because whatever you say is a sign of your madness.

It's ironic that the label of 'madness' itself causes the same kind of powerlessness, the same abusive wrenching-away of choice and freedom and autonomy, the same kind of shame and humiliation, that the original trauma did. As a child, no one took me seriously or believed me, listened to what I wanted, respected my body, treated me as if what I felt mattered. Being a 'psychiatric patient' is rarely any different.

But what is more than ironic—what in reality is a tragic human rights atrocity—is that the system of care called psychiatry in this country and much of the Western world is based upon 'treatment' for severe trauma which replicates the dynamics of that original abuse. Do we really, as a nation, think that in order to 'get better,' in order to recover from the distress of decades of abuse, we have to be treated as if we have no rights?—the right to be believed and listened to, the right to be in control of our life and our body? Should we be treated as if we have no value or worth? Why is it that to treat the effects of powerlessness, which is the core of so much trauma and abuse, psychiatry thinks that we should be powerless?

One of my indelible experiences of the last few years is seeing the backdraft of people withdrawing, unconsciously and imperceptibly perhaps at first, when I say that I have a 'mental health condition' or that I am a 'survivor of abuse.' Many people treat me instinctively as if I am dangerous, as if I am about to act in a bizarre or illogical way: 'No sudden movements—she startles easily!' More than anything, they don't want to talk about the reality of what my life has been, or is. On the whole I am welcome for dinner or lunch or to social gatherings as long as I don't say what I do, or how I am, or how I've been; as long as I don't talk about trauma or abuse or mental health or any of those oh-so-uncomfortable topics. The result is a deep sense of stigma and rejection: I am only acceptable as long as I act 'normal' and dissociate my trauma. Both 'madness' and suffering are unwelcome realities in our society.

So for me, the path of recovery has involved having to think differently about myself and my 'symptoms.' I'm not 'mad.' Not when the piercing scream inside can only be quietened with self-harm. Not when I act and talk and think as if I am five years old and believe that 'the nasty men are coming.' Not when I don't know where I've been for the last few hours and there is a cacophony in my head of squabbling voices. Not when I can't sleep, night after night after panic-ridden night. Not even when I feel sensations in my body that have no obvious cause, such as the tightness of ropes around my wrists, or burning in my genitals—things that objectively aren't there, but feel as if they are.

None of these experiences are 'symptoms' of mental disorder, of the brain gone wrong through some supposed 'chemical imbalance' or organic disease. They are just the traumas of my childhood, the jigsaw pieces which my mind didn't have space or capacity to process at the time, coming out of the box and finding their way, bit by bit, into the picture that is my life. The process of recovery has been delayed every time I have discarded one of those pieces as being just a bizarre, illogical sign of 'madness.' It feels terribly shameful to accept that these experiences are actually logical, that I was actually abused, that these memories are mine, and so are these beliefs and thoughts and voices. But that is a shame that society has put on me for being apparently 'mad' *and* a survivor of sexual abuse; it is not a shame that belongs to me.

The process of recovery is an individual one. There are a lot of discarded jigsaw pieces that each one of us has to pick up, turn around, examine, fit in. But it is made all the harder by living in a society where we are stigmatised, rejected and shamed for being 'nutters' who ought to be locked away in psychiatric wards, away from public view. Certainly it would be easier on society that way—they wouldn't have to face up to the prevalence of trauma and abuse in our oh-so-civilised country, or their complicity by operating on a 'see no evil, hear no evil' basis as the Jimmy Savile case has so abundantly made clear.

But society needs to want to do more than 'treat' us by drugging us so that we can't remember the trauma anymore, so that we can't feel the distress anymore. Society needs to let us grieve and reorganise and reorder our lives and come to terms with what happened to us, and with what our families were or were not, and support us in the process.

That process, what I'm calling here 'recovery,' might involve a lot of 'crazy' behaviour as we stare into space or cry uncontrollably or fail to turn up for work or do a thousand other things that make perfect sense when we understand the context. But we are not 'crazy': not us, as individuals. It is all of us together, corporately, as a society that are 'crazy': this society that churns out adults who abuse children with such impunity and lack of remorse; this society that builds 'crazy,' dissociative structures in our healthcare system that denies us appropriate help and support as budget-anxiety shifts responsibility to another department. That, in fact, may be the greater, the more traumatic realisation—that we weren't abused because we were bad, and toxic, and sick, but because society as a whole is. Perhaps we need to take the label off us as individuals as being 'bad' or 'mad' and start looking, every one of us, at what we each need to do—for we are all part of this 'crazy' society—to develop a more compassionate, caring, remorseful, empathic, non-violent way of living together.

Importantly, we won't do that if we don't remove our 'mad/bad' label, because we won't have the courage to speak up, and we will allow our label to silence us. Who listens to a 'mad' person?! The first and the best thing we can do to contribute towards a saner society is to start to recover, and to demand by our very survival that we are treated with dignity and respect, not with stigmatising labels and sometimes-irrelevant diagnoses. Recovery will always be, in my mind, the best revenge for what happened to us.

So I'm not mad. I'm not bad. I'm just traumatised. And I'm recovering.

CHAPTER THREE

Ten reasons I didn't tell

1.   No one asked.
Maybe if someone had asked me a direct question, I would have given them a direct answer. But no one ever did. I sidled up to a teacher once in my PE kit and stretched out my hands, but she didn't see. Or at least, she didn't ask. I looked deep into the wonderings of the Avon lady but she never wondered out loud, and never to me. I tried sitting next to my friend's Mum on the coach on the school trip to London, but she only talked about the traffic. It wouldn't have mattered if the Doctor had asked, because my Mum was always sitting right next to me and I could only semaphore nakedly with my eyes. It wasn't worth the risk anyway. Never mind.

2.   I didn't know it was happening.
It's difficult to talk about something that you don't know is happening. The day child, the night-time child; the indoor child, the outdoor child; the happy child, the unhappy child. If only they could have met: there would have been so much to say. The necessity of dissociation at the time makes it difficult to communicate apart from the dysfunction of fragmented emotion. My communication with a world that didn't listen was through illness, pain, sleepwalking and the occasional outburst of bizarrely inappropriate behaviour such as chasing down

an old couple who got it wrong at a T-junction and nearly pranged me in my mother's car; I didn't understand why I suddenly wanted to kill them for just an innocent mistake, and they certainly didn't. After they pulled in terror into a police station car park to evade me, I returned home hot-faced and confused. I didn't know I was reacting out of transference because I didn't know what had been happening the night before (and I certainly didn't know what transference was).

3. They told me not to tell and I wanted to be good.
It might seem odd to want to be good by not telling, but adults had told me not to tell and being a child I had no rational powers to determine if they could be disobeyed. I wanted to be good. Good in order to be safe—yes; but good to be *good*. I didn't want to be like them. I wanted to be good. And I had been told not to tell. So telling would have been disobedient, naughty, and bad. And I wasn't going to do that if I could help it.

4. They told me not to tell and said they would kill me if I did.
It might seem reasonable to believe their threat but as adults I suppose we would tend to dismiss it as just that—a threat—and rationalise that a child could know no better than to believe it. But it wasn't just a threat. When you have seen them kill another child your age—perhaps your age, perhaps even younger—you believe them utterly when they say that they will kill you. You believe without questioning that *they will know* if you gulp too loudly in assembly at school. And you live every day with the *knowledge* that it will be your turn next and there is no point—ever—in planning too far ahead. Telling would only quicken the suicide.

5. There was no one to tell.
When you look around the playground, you can't be sure if you have seen those faces elsewhere, in the terror of crackling candle-light; you wouldn't want to tell someone who might tell that you've told. And the adults in your life—the teachers, the nit nurse, the friends of your parents—were *they* there, are *their* faces fire-flickering familiar? There

was no one, afterwards, to help clean up the blood; there is certainly no one—*no one*—to tell.

6.   I deserved what was happening.

It never occurred to me that this might not be so. It has always happened, as long as memory has stretched backwards; it will always happen, as long as anticipation stretches forward. Its genesis is in my soul-intrinsic evil; good things happen to good girls and there's no experimental parallel universe in which to test out alternative hypotheses: *this* is reality. Words that form the wallpaper of my mind, whispered or commanded or bellowed by my abusers, tell me it is so, and *it is so*. I deserve it; I have caused it; I *am* it.

7.   No one would believe me.

They said no one would believe me. An itchy cloth against my mouth, eye-stinging smells, rushing head… I can't remember what happened next, so who will believe me? At school I write stories, paint pictures: fantastical, allegorical, metaphorical, but never (assume the teachers) *true*. They don't believe I'm not hungry (have another potato), don't believe I don't want to play out (out you go anyway), don't believe I'm feeling poorly (there's nothing wrong with you), so why should they believe about knives and sticks and ropes and ditches and water and *dead?* Of course it's not true. Those things don't happen to anyone *we* might know. And certainly not in England.

8.   No one would have done anything about it.

If a group of adults can stand and watch while you are raped and not intervene, what makes you think that anyone else will help? And if, having tried once, maybe twice, to tell one, maybe both, of your parents, and having been shouted at, and smacked, then tortured, for doing so—what makes you think that anyone else will do anything to stop it?

9. I didn't want anyone to know.

I am Bad, Unspeakable, Filthy and Vile. I do things that only adults do, I have murdered, I am *shit*. I don't want people to hate me. I don't want to go to prison. I don't want to be rejected. I don't want to be so naughty. Why would I want anyone to know about the things that I can't even bear to know myself?

10. I didn't have the words to tell.

Just once or twice I saw some kind eyes, eyes that seemed to lean right into me and offer peace, safety, warmth. And I tried to lean back into them, to tell, to speak, to say. But I didn't have the words. I didn't know what the problem was, I didn't have a lexicon. And back, back in time—reaching through the cot with pleading eyes of terror—I didn't have *any* words then and I couldn't even point. By the time the first brave crude words started to come, the kind eyes had leaned away and the moment was gone and the moment would not return.

CHAPTER FOUR

I hate me: the logic of self-hate

I hate me. Three words, and my frequent assertion. I've stopped saying it now as 'adult me' but it's a predictable refrain still from other parts of myself.

I hate me. It's not just a statement. It's a warhead of painful emotion. It's a summary of everything bad in my life, all the yuk stuff that has happened to me, that I've been part of, that I've lived through and tried at times to die through, squeezed down into three words.

I hate me. There's something dissonant about it though, as if it's an echo of something I remember. It's as if they are someone else's words, someone else's mindset, contorted and funnelled through my lips.

I hate me. I didn't grow up to decide one day to hate myself. It doesn't work like that. In fact, it's almost the opposite of that. I grew up hating myself and one day, in therapy, I realised that that's what I was doing. It was so normal to me, so natural, like air and sunlight and the twittering of birds, that I hadn't noticed it. It just was. Then came this abrupt collision in my mind, of a therapist pointing out that I hated myself and I didn't have to anymore.

I hate me. It's difficult to shift. When it's first pointed out, it makes it worse: I hate me for hating me. Now I'm a failure all over again. Now I'm abnormal, a freak, dysfunctional, and there's something else been added to my list of all the things I need to change about me, all the things I need to work on and address, all the things I need to mould somehow into a different way of being.

I hate me. I didn't even know why I hated me. I just did. It seemed obvious. Doesn't everyone? No, not everyone does. Some people seem to have this lightness and this ease, a way of being with themselves that isn't steeped in self-loathing, in malice and disgust, a way of being like the delicacy of voile, the freshness of Spring air, the comfort of warm porridge. I knew that some people were different. Most wouldn't understand that feeling of putrid, sticky hatred that makes you want to cut yourself apart, burn yourself, hang yourself, smother yourself to death. It comes like a tidal wave of unexpected ferocity, triggered by something as ordinary as a glimpse in a mirror. It is literally a flood: no other thoughts remain, no other feelings, just this overflow of sewage bursting up through the manhole covers of my self.

I hate me. It's painful too. A kindness, a look, a gesture, a comment: soft eyes that aren't filled with hatred, looking at me with compassion and care, elicit a pain so physical, so real, so unbearable, that everything in me recoils and yelps as if we've been burnt with fire. It hurts when someone doesn't hate me. Maybe it stirs in me the longing for unhate. Maybe it reminds me of the awfulness of hate. Whatever it is, not being hated *hurts*.

I hate me. It doesn't have a single source. It's an aggregation of thousands of tiny moments of uncare, of neglect, of emptiness, of isolation and despair, all gunged together by the stickiness of hundreds of individual acts of extreme violence and hatred and abuse. It's intrinsic to us, like the skin on our body.

I hate me. Aaah, the body. That's a source of hatred too—a source and an object. Our body is a sponge for hatred. It's the interface between our soul and our abusers. It's this medium, this vehicle, this bridge over which the abuse was enacted. Our body was a source of shame, and pain, and dis-ease. We may not mean to blame it for the abuse, but it is tarnished by association. It is barely comprehensible to us that our bodies could be a source of pleasure, and an object of care. Our bodies express our emotions—forbidden emotions, that betray us, like tears or panic or nausea. Our bodies have this direct, almost innocent way, of displaying what is happening on the inside of us. And that is disallowed and to be feared, so we battle constantly with our bodies to coerce them into disingenuous obedience. They *will not* betray us.

I hate me. And I'm weary with hating me. It takes up so much energy. There's no strength left for anything else. We use our hatred to guard ourselves from doing wrong, like a schoolmaster and cane. If everything that happened to us was our fault, then our self-hatred can at least guard us from doing it again. If there is any risk of pleasure, or success, or love, or peace, then our self-hatred can sabotage it so that we don't stray into such dangerous territory again.

I hate me. But maybe it's time for a change. Maybe I could try on a new suit of emotions. Maybe I could risk not hating me. Maybe I could try compassion and care, kindness and love. It's what I want for other people: why not for me? Maybe hating is old hat now. Maybe it's the way things used to be. Maybe I don't need it. Maybe it doesn't need me. Maybe I can trust myself not to hate me anymore, maybe I can believe that I'm safe. I don't know what to replace it with but it's irking me, irritating me, discomforting me. What could I do instead? What could I do instead of *I hate me?*

Maybe I won't hate me anymore.

CHAPTER FIVE

You think I'm crazy?! Think again!
My dissociative thought life

I'm looking at him, and he's looking right back, and we've both got that 'I can't believe you said that!' look on. All I said was, 'Well, anyway... I don't even know if I've got DID...' and he's trying not to say anything, to let the craziness of what I've just said sink in, but he's also got that *other* look on, the one that says, 'Can't you see what you're doing?'

So we have The Conversation. Again. And by the end of it, I can see the utter logic of what he's saying to me, that with DID 'denial of the syndrome is part of the syndrome,' that yes I was abused, however much I wish I wasn't and want to believe in the myth of the happy childhood; that yes I do have DID, as evidenced by a hundred tiny symptoms as well as the huge, ridiculously-over-obvious ones; and that yes it's because I've been touching trauma in my therapy sessions lately and this is the pattern that I always fall into when feelings start to hit—of pushing it all away with denial, of sidestepping that cacophony of painful emotions by attacking myself instead for 'making it all up.'

Bother. Like any wife, I hate it when my husband is right.

Denial tugs away at me day in, day out. Mostly nowadays I'm familiar with its cunning attacks, the way that it seeks to defend me from unbearable reality by whispering its sweet seduction that nothing happened, that I don't have DID, that I'm making it all up. But then, not so sweetly, comes its more coercive tactic, and suddenly I'm attacking *myself* for being this evil, twisted, insane-without-a-reason maniac who just invents stories for attention and has been stringing along both husband and therapist for over six years now. When I *really* stare it in the face, I realise that I have everything to gain but also everything to lose by accepting the distorted reality that denial offers me: so hey I wasn't abused after all, and that's a huge relief, but I am also irrevocably deranged for 'creating' all these post traumatic symptoms, when there's no trauma to be 'post.' But depressing though that position is, it's also strangely comforting, because it confirms in me my core belief that I am *bad*, that I am *evil* and that I am *mad*. And then suddenly, and strangely, all is well with the world again, because I've re-established the internal *status quo* where life makes sense: where all the guilt for all the evil in all the world lies within *me*, and where the abuse (if it happened at all) was *my* fault, and I deserved it. And of course all the difficulties that I face in adult life on a daily basis now are well-earned punishments for the toxic clump of unutterable badness that I am, deep within the core of my being, far beneath the normal-looking, normal-acting, just-be-nice exterior.

And this brings me to the subject of crazy thinking. As I've said in various ways in various articles, overt 'multiple personalities' are not all there is to dissociative identity disorder. For me, and for many people I know, 'crazy thinking' is a massive factor too. And that 'crazy thinking' is wrapped around a fundamental core of denial—denial of the trauma, and denial of the existence of 'parts' or 'alters' and all they represent. And on top of it lies layers of thick, oozy, self-hating beliefs about being bad, deserving abuse, needing to be punished. And let's not even go there with the impossibility of being loved.

You see, nothing bad happened *to me*: the badness is *in me*, not in things that did or didn't happen. I am just simply, purely and ineffably *bad*. So don't come near me, don't care for me, don't love me, and certainly don't try to like me. I am worthless, lazy, inept, selfish, wrong, needy, faithless and untrustworthy. I emanate toxicity, like a radioactive isotope. The problem is me: not the abuse, not the neglect, not the trauma, not the DID. The simplest explanation for everything in life is that *I am bad*.

Phew. Well that said it, didn't it? Now I need to beat a hasty retreat and scurry back into my normal-seeming, normal-sounding, normal-looking adult persona. Because that little outburst sounds an awful lot like the deranged mumblings of someone who also thinks that they're a cat. Or maybe an articulated lorry. The kind of person that really ought, for the benefit and protection of society, to be locked away in a lunatic asylum far far away from any Nimby's potential school-run. Because being as unhinged as I obviously am is probably going to require a shed-load of drugs and maybe a straitjacket to keep me in order.

The problem is that almost everyone that I've met who has a dissociative disorder, when they've been able to dare to say it, admits that they think this crazy stuff too. And we actually seem quite normal on the outside; some of us even manage to contribute positively to society, albeit usually *in spite of* a shed-load of drugs, rather than because of them. Self-loathing about our innate badness, as a defence against the awfulness of trauma inflicted upon us as children, is a common strategy for people who have been traumatised. With 'disorganised attachment patterns' we believe not just that we are bad, but that the world is dangerous too: it's a bleak outlook on life and so much of what goes on in our heads we daren't admit to another human being. The only thing that seems to keep me from the straitjacket and padded cell is that I can notice those thoughts in my head, think about them, and choose not to act on them—at least most of the time. The 'multiplicity' that is inherent in DID is probably what helps: I'm used to having more than one stream of consciousness at a time, more than one usually contradictory set of thoughts rotating in my mind. I am used to the warring of voices in my head, one of them saying, 'We're bad,' another retorting, 'No we're not.' On the walls inside my head, it's all colours and stripes and flashing neon lights; it's all weird perspectives and strobe lighting and Damien Hirst. The shock for me is when I meet someone whose mental wallpaper is plain magnolia and when they only manage to think one thought at a time. That does seem rather peacefully attractive.

But most 'normal' people do also maintain some level of mental chatter in their heads. Even 'normal' people are used to their inner voices that scold them for cracking a stupendous unfunny in front of a group of peers. Most people can recognise the runaway train of thoughts before they have to stand up and present in public, that disjointed, panicky spaghetti of thoughts that rarely progress beyond 'But I can't!' Getting a grip on your negative self-talk is standard fare in self-help books: it's certainly not limited to the world of DID.

So in that sense, what I experience in my mind is on the same spectrum as other people. But my self-talk and mental meanderings exist at the more extreme end of the spectrum, and tackling them, challenging them, learning to engage with them and not always *believe* them, has been a major part of my healing journey. It was spectacularly important for me to recognise at an early point that just because I feel something, it doesn't make it true. Reality is not determined by my feelings. I can feel something strongly without it being based in actuality; I can also *think* something, and believe it, without it being true. Feelings and thoughts are things that go on on the inside of me; they are sometimes responses to my environment, but often they are responses through the filter of trauma and dissociation. My thoughts and my feelings are not always the best guides for me to follow, at least not on their own and without further corroborating evidence.

So I have had to learn to 'notice' my feelings, to think about my thoughts, to recognise that they are things that happen in my head, but that they are not the totality of my consciousness. Feelings have this habit of coming and then going; sometimes they are numbed out and puzzlingly out of reach; at other times they sizzle and pop with ferocious intensity. But then they pass. The same is true of thoughts. Thoughts and feelings are merely activities of part of my mind, and I can step back and observe them rather than believing that everything they say is true. I can feel crazy because my thoughts and feelings so often contradict each other, but that's just the result of trauma, not any innate insanity. And I have come to realise that my crazy thinking operates in four distinct territories: self-deprecation; danger; managing anxiety; and distancing and denial.

Firstly, self-deprecation. These are the core beliefs of innate badness that I have already mentioned: I am evil, I am toxic, I am damaged, I am unloveable, I don't belong, I am weak, I am worthless, I am incompetent, I am foolish, I can't do people, I can't succeed, I can't get better, I can't cope. You see, the list is long and this is just a summary. And then the blaming: everything that happened was my fault as a child ('If only I hadn't gone there,' 'I should have run away') and it's a pattern which has continued snakily into today: 'I'm sorry' as the constant refrain for life; taking the blame for everything that *other people* do wrong, not just myself; feeling like I'm getting in the way, that I'll get into trouble, that I'll make people cross; that I should do better, that it's me that got it wrong; that I'm the cause of everyone else's difficulties and emotions.

Not all of these thoughts are constant, and not all of them are believed. But I hear them as a chorus in my head, different voices speaking from different perspectives, different parts or aspects of myself holding fundamentally contradictory thoughts and beliefs at the very same time. This is the essence of the conflict that is at the core of DID: multiple 'internal working models,' multiple views of the world, the self and others, all co-existing in a complex interplay of real-time contradiction. At the same time that a part of me thinks, 'It's my fault,' another part of me can think, with deeply-held conviction, 'No it's not.' That contradiction is confusing to live with; the raucous babble of clashing viewpoints makes it difficult at times to find within myself a stable sense of 'This is who I am; this is what I think; this is what I believe.' And not surprisingly, blaming voices of self-deprecation seem to dominate: negativity rules.

This kind of thinking takes effort and time to shift, and lots of it. It's a bit like dieting: it takes a long time to see any progress, and there are numerous temptations to give up *en route* because 'it's not working.' I have grappled, both in therapy and on my own, with my 'cognitive distortions,' the ways of thinking that I have grown up with that are a little off-key, somewhat skew-whiff. It has always felt inaccurate to say that I have a 'negative filter,' as sometimes I am risk-lovingly positive and not averse to seeing the world as full of illimitable possibilities. I have come to accept that I have a filter, as everyone does, but it is more precise to call it a 'trauma filter.' I see everything through the eyes of what happened to me as a child, even while I am stubbornly denying that my history includes abuse. So the world is tinged with powerlessness, coercion, pain, and humiliation: it is not always a happy place to live in.

This can spill into my everyday activities, and means that I can see risk where it is not, see threat where it is not, see malice where it is not. I have been challenged to look for the evidence: I have been confronted with the reality that I cannot actually mind-read other people, that I need to ask them what is going on in their head rather than jumping to conclusions about their malevolent appraisal of me. I have to constantly acknowledge that there are other reasons for people's actions beyond my existence: sometimes they haven't replied to an email because they are busy, not because I have offended them. I have to stop myself jumping to premature conclusions, or focusing only on the negative, believing it's a case of all-or-nothing, black-or-white, yes-or-no. I have to force myself to zoom out, consider things from a wider perspective rather than the narrowed-down myopic anxiety that often ends up in catastrophic predictions: 'I can't do it,' 'It won't work,' 'I'll only fail,' 'Everything is going to go wrong.'

Then there is the issue of danger. My husband does not live with a danger mindset. As a result (or so I say in order to prove the value of my terrorised standpoint) he has had two mobile phones stolen, because it doesn't occur to him that the people around him are likely to do bad things like stealing. Especially not when they are Year 8 children in a classroom, who ought to be listening to him explain the fascinations of respiration. I however do live with a danger mindset and I have never had a mobile phone stolen. That is the only positive I can derive from having experienced the terrors I did as a child. But it also shows the flipside of what we usually consider to be a negative symptom of a traumatised past: hypervigilance.

Being on high alert all the time is exhausting; it has many downsides. But it is not something that we can just switch off. Trauma has caused actual structural changes in our brains, a rearrangement of our internal head furniture which means that we are more sensitive than others to certain cues in the environment. A lot of this is centred around a tiny part of the brain called the amygdala, what is often referred to in metaphorical terms as the 'smoke detector' of the brain. Most of the sensory information that is constantly zinging into the brain ends up in the amygdala, and within around 7 milliseconds the 'smoke alarm' assesses it for threat. It's as if it's sniffing it and checking it out for smoke. If, based on previous patterns and experiences, this muddle of data smells 'smoky,' then the alarm is set off. The amygdala initiates the body's arousal systems and there is an immediate increase in heart rate, breathing, blood pressure and blood sugar levels in order to prepare to deal with this supposed threat. Welcome to life with a dissociative disorder—and you wondered why we're jumpy?!

That's all well and good if the house is on fire. But what if it's just a case of burnt toast? Unfortunately for us as trauma survivors, our 'smoke detector' can become oversensitive. It was in too many fires as a child, and so it has a tendency to assume the worst: that wisp of smoke might be the next Great Fire of London rather than the wick burning on a well-guarded candle. And the amygdala, quite out of conscious thought, before we've even had a chance to think and choose our reaction, sets off our alarm responses. All the time. That's why we get triggered so easily; that's why we live with this constant, danger-scanning tension. That's why many of us want to sit with our back to the wall in a bar or restaurant so we can keep an eye on everything and everyone who is coming and going. Watching out for threat is a learned response. We notice things that have changed, things that are new, things that have disappeared, and we interpret them as warning signals of danger because of the way that our brain has been wired through trauma to assume the worst—to give us the maximum possible time to react and respond and escape this imminent blaze.

And then our thoughts get muddled up with it too. The feedback we are getting internally, from this over-sensitive smoke alarm, is telling us that everything around us is dangerous. And so the thoughts start rolling in: is our therapist out to hurt us too? She has been nice to us, has paid us attention: some of the things that abusers did, *right before they hurt us.* So what's different now? Just being in the same room as her is astonishingly stressful. Sometimes our thoughts race around like puppies in our mind: *Why did she do that? What's the right answer?*

Am I going to be in trouble? The greatest risk to us sometimes is the risk of intimacy and vulnerability. And our minds roil with scenarios of imagined danger, based on patterns from the past.

Closely connected to this is the way that our minds churble with anxiety, and we employ a thousand discrete strategies to manage it. For some this is the realm of obsessive compulsive disorder: I am definitely on the spectrum, but not at the diagnosable end. I like things to be in straight lines. I like there to be order, for things to be tidy, for things to 'make sense.' Visually, in publications, I need the fonts to be clean, the alignments to be accurate, the colours to match. The wrong font—Comic Sans is the most evil of culprits—can make me nauseous with a sense of 'wrongness.' There has to be consistency, the same rules applied to all, discrepancies smoothed out. Recent research hints that it's my dACC, my dorsal anterior cingulate cortex, that is to blame, that it is hyperactive in its pattern-matching, that it emits a warning signal to the smoke alarm if things don't quite add up. In practice, my thoughts whirr with apprehensive longing for order and conformity. I *need* to straighten the papers on my desk before I can think about writing another sentence. I am distracted by the folders falling over each other on my bookcase. And my unspoken belief is that *if I can just straighten that, if I can just clean off that fluff, if I just empty my bin,* then life will be manageable. In reality, these odd little compulsions never go away, are never satisfied. Instead, they tend to multiply as they become the promised panacea to all our fears. For some people, it's about doing things in patterns of four, washing their hands to obsessive levels of cleanliness, touching the doorframe in the same place with their hand, or the threshold with their foot. It's a mental melée. It's day-to-day life for many of us with a dissociative disorder.

And finally, distancing and denial. I've said it already. But in the time that it has taken to write this, I have veered wobbily in and out of denial another half dozen times. It's as if there is a man with a shovel in my mind. As soon as any pain amasses, as soon as emotions start piling up against the edges of my brain, out comes this little man with his denial-spade, to dig away at my reality. *Was I abused? How do I know I was? What if I wasn't? What if I made it all up? What if I didn't?* Round and round and round we go and soon I'm dizzy with the argument and I've forgotten the pain that accepting and confronting the trauma had brought me. It's such a clever distraction. It's so constant. It's as if a part of my head goes blank, and there is simply void where there used to be reason. And I gulp with panic because *I've made it all up* and in the silence of the void where the man has been digging with his denial-spade, there is no reply. And five minutes can pass where I sit in bewildered repulsion at myself for having concocted the entirety of my trauma history, my symptoms, my life. Catastrophic thinking kicks in… *What am I going to do? How am I going to put this right? Everyone will hate me!*… and sometimes just in time—just before the point at which I lose all sense of yes and no and me and I—the truth eases back in like the tide and I remember again that there's logic in my trauma history, and none without. But in the meantime I've intellectualised all the emotion away, and so I can say, 'Yes, bad things happened to me,' but I don't need to feel it, because denial has distracted me for another half-day.

This is what it is like so much of the time: mental scuffles, marauding thoughts, terror-edged denial. My thoughts, and the feelings they elicit, can be chaotic, irrational, *mad*. And all of this goes on below the surface, out of sight, where no one can see, so that no one will spot the fact that I'm quite as mad as I am, and I-as-adult-me can fulfil my role of acting normal. The battle with our minds is one of the biggest ones with DID. Often we don't voice what is going on for us, because there are too many contradictions. 'How was your week?' is an innocent question, but how do we respond? *It was fine. No it wasn't. It was good. It was awful. Why is she asking? Nothing much happened. We were ill for two days solid. It was ok. I wanted to die. We had a pretty good week really. I can't remember my week at all. What's the right answer? Don't mention Tuesday night. How was yours?* And every one of those responses, every one of those viewpoints and experiences and reflections, would be true.

Am I crazy? Not really. But my thoughts often are. I have a developmental brain disorder: I have struggled to connect up all the individual strands of existence that have been mine, and to twine them together into a sense of self that is unified, and whole. I have segregated off parts of my experience that have been too traumatic or overwhelming. And sometimes that disowned experience comes crashing back into my mind with all the ferocity of needful overprotectiveness, shouting at me not to trust, not to get too close, not to say, not to feel. Slowly I am gathering these shredded parts of me together, trying to develop some give-and-take, conversationally, into my mind. Sometimes it's hard not to catastrophise, to over-focus on a negative, to think I can mind-read another, to magnify mine or others' faults, to slip into all-or-nothing, black-and-white thinking.

'It's denial again,' he says, with *that* look on his face—a mixture of frustration and deep, deep compassion. And I have to admit that he's right, that my thoughts have been whizzing around like cars on a Nascar track, because yesterday in therapy I glimpsed some feelings that are way way too painful to feel. He's helping me ground again, to get back to that place where I can both think *and* feel, where it's not all too much and my thoughts don't have to rev up their engines in order to escape from the pain. 'You're right, I say,' resigned at last. But because I don't want to accept total defeat and I need to leave room for manoeuvre in the future, I have to—just *have to*—add, with a cheeky smile, 'But I still deny that I have a problem with denial.'

CHAPTER SIX

Ten things I have learned about child sexual abuse

My earliest memory is of being sexually abused in a big, old-fashioned cot in a room with ornate, mock-gold picture frames and ornaments of shire horses and Greek gods. I was two years old, maybe three. If that's when I first *remember*, what was happening prior to that? I will never know. It continued until I was 16 or 17 when one of the perpetrators moved out of the home.

This is my history, but I have struggled to come to terms with it. My mind protected me by dissociating, for decades shutting off the trauma into non-memory. When the dissociative amnesia began to peel away, I rejected those memories because I didn't understand them, and not understanding them, I denied they were mine. But I have come to understand that the experiences I had are common experiences, albeit they were crimes. The survival strategies I employed are common strategies, albeit they led to dissociative identity disorder. And the post-traumatic symptoms I developed are a syndrome of symptoms, albeit that society would rather blame me for them by labelling me 'mad.'

I was abused in the home, outside the home, in organised groups, in settings that had a ritualised element to them, by people I knew and by people I did not. I was abused by men, by women, and by adolescents. The impact has been huge, but bit by bit I am building a life free of flashbacks, one that is attempting to draw together the many strands of my experience. I have disowned these strands, distancing myself from them. But now I am trying to integrate them together into a coherent whole, so that *I can* become a coherent whole, with a coherent narrative and a coherent understanding of who I am.

I am a 'survivor' of child sexual abuse in the very best sense of the word. We can and we do survive. Understanding the dynamics around child sexual abuse, who the perpetrators are, how they achieve their ends, the impacts of abuse on us—all of this knowledge, this 'psycho-education' has aided my recovery. And so these are ten of the many things that I have learned about child sexual abuse, some of the insights that have begun to heal my shame.

1. Flashbacks won't kill you, and they are your mind trying to heal.

I felt that I was going crazy. It was hard not to: my mind would flood, suddenly, unexpectedly, with images and repulsion and terror and dread. At all times, in all ways, the staccato interruptions of half-memories and body sensations would puncture my existence. I hated it. I wanted more than anything for it to stop, for my mind to return to normal, for the boxes in my head to stack neatly again and not divulge their contents. It was overwhelming. A noise, a sensation, a thought... and suddenly I am assaulted by eye-scratching images of abuse. The steel-hard reality of normality around me fades and I am *back in it,* reliving it, as real in my body as it was back then. I feel pain, disgust, terror. I retch or crumple, even pass out. These experience were overwhelming and they were continual. Dozens of times a day, every day of the week, for years. I'm not quite sure how I survived.

It was much later in my recovery that I realised that flashbacks weren't the enemy. The flashbacks were my mind trying to heal. It was trying to connect up the dots, fill in the gaps, make sense of this squabble of experiences that I'd tried, as hard as I could, to keep out of mind. But my mind veers relentlessly towards truth. It can only dissociate and avoid for so long. It is pre-programmed to recover. And these flashbacks, distressing and debilitating though they were, were my mind's insistence that we wouldn't live in the shadows any longer. We were going to bring this thing into the light, and we were going to deal with it. And then we would be free of it. I have come to believe that the symptoms of child sexual abuse are the beginnings of recovery. When it starts to affect us, that is a good sign. We are going to heal.

2. 'Monsters don't get close to children—nice people do.'
These are the words of the late Ray Wyre, a respected child sexual abuse investigator. The concept of the stranger in the mac jumping out from the bushes is a stereotype and myth. The vast majority of children who are sexually abused know their abuser. Our children are more at risk from within the family than they are from without. But we don't want to know that. We want the reassuring image of the sick paedophile, the monster. Then we will know who to watch out for. The idea of sex offenders dressed in Next and driving a Golf is too disturbing for us. So we force it out of mind and welcome instead the stereotype, because that is easier to live with.

So *everyone* dissociates. Everyone pushes unwelcome truth out of their mind. And this most unwelcome of truths is that respectable people abuse children. Accountants do, and bricklayers, and people who work on the tills at Tesco's. All sorts of people. And we can't tell who they are by looking at them.

When I considered the people who abused me, I struggled to accept it largely because they weren't evil all the time. They did normal things too. They ate, they laughed, they sang whilst baking shortbread. They did everything that everyone else—people who didn't abuse children—did. So I kept on refusing to believe that they had abused me too. For many years, I wanted the image more than I wanted the truth, because the truth is painful. The truth is that nice people are not always nice and that 'monsters' live in four-bedroomed houses too.

3. The tools of the abusers are denial, minimisation and blame.
But we hurt ourselves when we use these tools too.
To abuse a child, you need to distort the truth. Because the truth is hideous, and your actions are crimes. So abusers employ 'the triad

of cognitive distortion.' Firstly, they deny altogether that they are abusing. They tut at the television when such things are mentioned, and deny even to themselves that they are engaged with the same. *I'm not doing anything wrong. This isn't abuse.* But if truth is too forcefully imposed on their situation, then they move on to minimisation. *It's not hurting anyone. It's not that bad. It's not like it's rape or anything. It's only a bit of fun. I'm only looking. It's my way of showing affection.* If that doesn't work, then they resort to blame. *It's not my fault. She made me do it. She (or he) started it. It's what he (or she) wanted.*

In this way abusers avoid facing their crimes. In this way they shirk responsibility for the hurt they are causing. But it damages us further when we employ these tactics too. If by dissociating we deny that we were ever abused—*It didn't happen to me; it happened to another part of me*—or we deny that it bothers us—*It's no big deal, worse things happened to other kids*—or we take the blame for it ourselves—*It's because I was bad, and I deserved it*—then we will drown in the abuser's cesspit of lies. Recovery involves facing the truth, knowing the truth, letting the truth seep deep into our bones, and rejecting the reality imposed on us by the perpetrators. It's not our shame; it's theirs. It's not our guilt; it's theirs. It's not our fault; it's theirs. It is a scary thing to place the responsibility back where it belongs, on our abusers— especially if they are also our family—but unless we do it then we are colluding with the denial, minimisation and blame that they used to hurt us, and we are missing the chance to heal.

4. Child sexual abuse is something that happened to me, but it does not define who I am.

The impact of abuse runs right to my core. The experiences I had as my brain was first forming lay templates for me for the rest of my life. I assume I am bad, and toxic, and unloveable, because that is what I was told and how I was treated. The experience of abuse has at times completely entwined me, like Russian vine around a pergola. But recovery comes through recognising that I was a person before I was abused. I was a person during the abuse. And I am a person now, after the abuse. The abuse is something that was imposed upon me, like whitewash on a building. However deeply I have felt contaminated to the very foundations of my self, in reality it is external. It does not define who I am. It says more about my abusers than it does about me.

I struggled at first to accept that I had suffered child sexual abuse, to identify myself as a victim of such monstrous crimes. I had to own those experiences which previously I had banished to the far reaches of my mind. I had to lay hold again of those memories, those beliefs, those thoughts, those feelings. But then I would disown them. And own them again. On and on in a spiral of ever-deepening rings. But eventually I could place those experiences outside of me, in a right way. *This is what someone did to me. It is not who I am. I am more than this. I am not the sum of my experiences. I am a person in my own right.* Having done that, it is easier to stand back from the trauma but still own it, to view the abuse as experiences I have had, rather than as determinants of my soul. Abuse defines the abusers more than it defines the victim.

5. The perpetrator grooms not just the victim but the family and society too

In grooming, the abuser prepares the victim to be abused. Resistance is eroded. Blame and responsibility creep onto the victim. Grooming protects the abuser and enables them to perpetrate, entrapping the victim with secrets, promises, threats and lies. *If you tell anyone, it will break up the family. You made me do this. I won't tell your mother you were drinking alcohol / taking drugs / skipping school / stealing biscuits. You're a naughty girl/boy for doing this, but I won't tell…* Grooming deeply distorts truth and inverts responsibility, leaving the victim deeply impacted in ways that can take years to unravel and heal. *It's my fault. I wanted it. Everyone does this. They love me. This is for my benefit. I caused this. I deserve this, because I am bad.* Grooming is about trickery and deceit, and recovery from its effects involves re-uniting with truth. But often that process is hampered because the wider network—the family, the church, the club, the school—have also been groomed. *She makes things up. He's trouble. I can babysit for you. Let me help you out. Doctors and teachers and police officers don't abuse.*

Society was groomed by Jimmy Savile. We believed his charity efforts. We smiled at his eccentricity. We succumbed to his power. Abusers groom everyone around them, inviting the belief that they are pillars of the community, the people whose version of events is *right*, the arbiters of truth. Sexual abuse doesn't happen in a vacuum. It happens in manufactured reality that abusers sometimes spend years creating. If you're willing to train to be a priest in order to gain access to children, or work in a nursery, or marry a single mother, then there's no limit to what you will do with that trust once you have it. That, sadly, is why abusers get away with it for so long. No one wanted to believe that Cyril Smith was anything other than fat. He was an MP. We have entrusted the country to men like him. So he is to be trusted. And children lie (or so they say).

6.   Powerlessness is the very essence of trauma, but we are powerless no longer

The freeze response makes sense. In the face of overwhelming threat, when fight and flight are no longer an option, a child—just like an antelope or a possum or a rabbit—freezes to survive. Perhaps she will escape detection. Perhaps it will numb the pain. Perhaps submission will win the day. The freeze response is a work of evolutionary genius, but it cramps our style. If we freeze when someone raises their voice, if we freeze when we spill a drink, if we freeze when someone walks behind us, then the freeze response is no longer adaptive. We need to update our mental maps, because we are no longer little and defenceless and unskilled. We are adults now, with resources we didn't have before, with the right to say no, with the right to be heard. We can develop our skills to amplify our no until it is heard and respected. We were powerless as children, and inevitably overwhelmed. But recovery is built on a new reality: we are no longer stuck; time has moved on; *we* have moved on. Powerlessness is a cage whose doors have opened, and we don't need to sit in it a moment longer. It takes time to learn this. It takes the dogged practice of every day, in some small way, *acting* rather than *freezing*. We need to build up new habits. But they are choices we are free to make now, and choices we need to make now if we are to emerge from the cocoon of victimisation, to spread our wings and fly.

7.   Remembering is not recovering

At the moment of trauma, our memory systems fail. The event is stored in our survival-based 'back brain,' a kinaesthetic and non-verbal imprint. In future, when faced with the same threat, we are primed to respond immediately and instinctually. It's clever, but it costs. Often then the event is not stored as a 'story' in our mind, the narrative explicit memory that composes our history. Instead the memory of abuse can be fuzzy, a barrage of body sensations and terror, not a neat bullet-point list of events. But it is all memory, and it is all valid. When our memory systems have been overrun by the cascade of stress hormones in our bloodstream, it makes remembering hard. We have the symptoms, we have the feelings, but we have no distinct story to tell. And so without a sense of history, we doubt if we can recover.

But remembering is not recovering. We can remember and still not recover. And we can recover without remembering. The indelible impression of trauma manifests itself in our symptoms and our behaviours: we jump at a sound, feel hopeless in the face of mild threat, flee at the faintest hum of conflict. Recovery is about relearning these reactions. The narrative is helpful because it explains the whys, making it easier for us to understand ourselves and accept compassion. But sometimes the narrative is just in our body and in our emotions, and that is enough to work with. So often we fear 'false memories' but ironically they exist most abundantly in abusers who declare that our childhood was perfect and that they were perfect parents too.

8.   Feelings are meant to be felt, and we can learn to adjust the volume

My home was a prison of avoidance where feelings were to be kept at bay: with dissociation, amnesia, alcohol, drugs, busyness, overwork. Feelings were my enemy. They obstructed my goals. They embarrassed me. They were unreliable, unpredictable. They were *bad*. My whole life was built around trying to avoid feelings, aiming for some nirvana where I could smile serenely with the wisdom of non-feel.

But feelings are meant to be felt. They are not meant always to be believed, or taken as the sole guide to action, or allowed to spit venom on the people around us. They are just meant to be felt. And having been felt, they will pass. But if they're ignored or repelled, they will keep coming back and clamour to be heard.

But feelings have a volume. Some of us try to keep that volume low, muted if possible, to walk uninterrupted through our day without the white noise of emotion. Others of us believe that our needs will be met if we ramp the knob up to 10, so our feelings drown out thought and reflection and the quiet, steady flow of relationship. Silent or ten. And in DID, those extremes are experienced within discrete parts of ourselves—alternate identities, some of whom are emotionally numb, whilst others are frantic with the scream of unremitting pain.

Abuse is distressing, and it ramped up the volume whilst muting it too: our abusers managed their feelings by overriding ours. So we learned to live in the silence, in the blare, from everything to nothing and back again, a thousand times a day. We couldn't find the volume knob to amplify the quiet, fluttery sounds in our tummy. And we couldn't turn it down either, away from the squawk of unrelenting distress. Recovery has involved feeling my feelings and using the volume knob—less out-of-control, dysregulated distress, and less numbed-out, avoidant, dissociative spaciness too. We can learn to live in the middle, accepting our feelings as part of us, part of what it means to be human, and part of life lived to the full where we feel positive feelings along with the negative ones.

9.   The stereotypes are inadequate

Women abuse. Boys are abused. Siblings abuse. Babies are abused. People in caring professions abuse. People with intellectual disabilities are abused. Parents abuse.

These are all true, but they are not the stereotype and so our lives bed down in shame that somehow our abuse was extraordinary, out of the range of normal human experience. We feel doubly bad for having been abused by a woman, by a mother, by an older sibling, by a *younger* sibling. But as we've seen already, the stereotypes serve society's denial and are not good indicators of truth. There is something indelibly shocking about a mother abusing a son, or even a mother abusing a daughter. It contradicts everything that we implicitly believe a mother to be. And when babies are abused, our attachment caregiving systems—that have evolved to nurture and protect the most vulnerable—scream with the horrifying wrongness of it. It happens, and more often than we care to believe. But I am not doubly bad for having suffered extreme abuse. There is nothing in *me* that caused it. I didn't deserve it. And there are thousands upon thousands of people like me, who also are trapped by the shame of this abuse. But it's more typical than any of us dare to believe, and it was all wrong, and it was all damaging, and you are not to blame.

10. We are survivors

Child sexual abuse causes very real damage—to our brains, to our personality development, to our 'internal working models,' even to our bodies' susceptibility to disease. Recovery is not swift. We need, in so many ways, to 'unlearn what we have learned.' We need to learn whom to trust and why. We need to develop skills for managing our feelings. We need to treat ourselves kindly, as worthy of self-care. We need to retrain our reactions and learn to handle flashbacks and triggers. We need to learn to relate well to others. We need to learn to assert ourselves in the face of someone else's power. These are hard tasks, but essential ones.

Healing doesn't come through denial or avoidance. It doesn't come through wearing a brave smile, and pretending that nothing happened. Healing doesn't come through perpetuating the lies of the abuser. Healing comes through embracing the truth.

But what is that truth? It is many things, but it includes the breathtaking triumph that we survived and we are still here. So many of us carry the shame posture of a victim, believing that we are weak and defective and worthless, but instead we should be proud. We are resilient. When we were defenceless and unsupported, mere children, we coped with intolerable pain, we coped with betrayal, we coped with deceit, and somehow we have kept on surviving. We are not pathetic—we are heroic.

If we can change our view of ourselves, if we can reframe our experiences as us surviving unbearable suffering, if we can see that we are creative and resourceful and determined and strong, then we will begin to heal. It is not what happened to us that matters so much as how we view it. We are not damaged goods. We are gold refined in a crucible. The challenge for us is to believe that this is so, and live our lives on the strength of who and what we really are, rather than the self-protective lies of our abusers. If we can do that, we can heal. And we *can* heal—more than anything, what I have learned about child sexual abuse is that it is not a death sentence, and it is not a life sentence. We can heal, and we can be free.

CHAPTER SEVEN

Dissociative moments

I am sitting at my desk, alone. But I don't feel alone. Everything is normal, but everything is different. There are sounds from the birds scrabbling on the roof. They are two metres above me, by the skylight. But they are far, far away. The walls are a pale yellow but their vibrancy seems to grab me. My eyes are sucking in their colour. I am falling back, deep down into myself. I am fuzzed in a fog. I am outside myself and deep within myself all at the same time. *I am having a dissociative moment.*

Moments like this happen all the time. Sometimes I know what has triggered them; at other times, it's a complete mystery. I feel myself floating. I feel as if everything around me has become unreal. I feel that I, myself, am unreal. Things that are familiar become unfamiliar. Characteristics, such as colours, or shapes, or the contrast of light against the dark, stand out and grab my attention as if I am looking through a tube at them: everything else fades away, and there is just this *one thing*, this one mostly irrelevant thing, this life-hanging-on-it *one thing* and I can't feel anything else or see anything else or do anything else but have my attention consumed by it.

Dissociative moments, falling into the mental fog, detaching from the body… And I don't always know what happens next. Sometimes it just dissolves and I'm back again, bewildered a little, feeling wrung-out, like I'm fumbling around on the inside to hang onto myself. I feel mentally dizzy, disoriented, like I've just stepped off a kids' roundabout. And always, *always*, the instinctive need to *act normal*, to try to make sure that no one has seen. The fear isn't that I dissociated; the fear is that someone noticed.

At other times I can't or I don't pull back from the brink, and I disappear inside. If I'm aware of it, it's like falling into sleep or an anaesthetic. Sometimes, when I'm inside, deep, deep down inside myself, I can see what's happening still on the surface. But I'm watching it from afar, and it's not me I'm watching. This is *co-consciousness*, the strangest feeling in the world. I can see myself talking and interacting and doing and feeling, and yet it's *not myself*, it's just someone else, someone I don't know, someone I have no connection with. And what they do and what they say surprises me. I don't know what's coming next. It just is. It just happens. And sometimes I hear my mouth saying things, and with thoughts crawling as if through glue, I think, deep inside, *No! Why are they saying that? What's going on?* And if it's too much then my thoughts just squash up into themselves and stop altogether and there's blank.

When I'm gone completely—when I've switched to another part, and I as me have lost contact altogether—then I only have the report of others to go on. That's when you see the most obvious signs of DID—an adult shifting perceptibly in the way we talk and hold our body and shift our eyes and interact with the world, until there is something so much evidently *younger* about us, or different in some other striking way: the angry, hostile side of us that you've never seen before; the emotion-spurting adolescent; the ragged, raw, empty *child-me*.

But me as *adult-me*: what do I know of my other selves? Six years ago, nothing. When I switched, I switched completely. I was gone, and nothing of what else I was in my other selves came through. Afterwards, when I was back, there was just a bustle of noise and prickly emotion in my head, all of it incomprehensible, like I had someone else's feelings and I didn't even know what they were. I relied on my husband or my therapist to tell me what I had been. They would describe the characteristics of my switch: a younger presentation of myself, traumatic memories blurting out in anguished distress, these parts all consumed in defending against some over-real threat. My husband or therapist would describe it to me, and I listened and accepted what they were saying as true, but in a detached, uninvolved way, as if they were recounting the plot of a film. It wasn't me they were describing. It wasn't relevant. It was curious, maybe embarrassing, but that was all. And too much information from them, too accurate a rendering of what I had been like, in a way that stirred a *connection* with what was deep inside me, and I would faze out again: this stuff was dissociated, disconnected and set apart for a reason, and the reason was because it was too painful, too conflictual, for me to know it. So they learned to tell me only slivers and were shocked by my insensitive, crass jocularity. 'A moment ago you were distraught, and now you're... *laughing?*' And I would shrug my shoulders because the distress was just an ominous discomfort inside, like psychological indigestion, and my laughter was an attempt to swallow it again.

Trauma intrudes continually. Not as much as it used to, now it has an outlet, but for years I didn't even know that trauma was its name. I walk down the High Street and suddenly pain spins up inside me like a corkscrew. I don't know why. I don't know what it is. Then nausea spurts up like a geyser. I'm dizzy, and suddenly everything around me feels unreal, all these people walking along in their unobtrusive, uncompanionable anonymity. They are unreal. I am unreal. Pain, nausea, and jarring echoes in my mind of *something*. A voice, deep inside me, that feels not-me but I know that it's not outside me: *Don't hurt me, don't hurt me.* And I realise that ten paces behind, a moment ago, was a man with a camera, and I can feel the fear inside, the wailing, the reluctant recoiling of a child part inside of me who was triggered by the man who walked past. A few more steps forwards, and it's past and I breathe again and I whisper inside to myself, *It's okay now, it's okay* and I remember to breathe and to zoom in on that breathing, in, out, *slowly now*, in, out, *it's okay*. And it passes and I'm back to adult, non-trauma life, back to the life that consists of a hundred of those intrusions every day. I can hold the hand of the little one inside me and I don't switch, I don't lose touch with my surroundings; I just hear the hurt and feel the pain and the nausea, for a moment, a long long moment sometimes, but then it is gone.

I used to think I was mad. Those jarring intrusions, those ego-alien, time-travelling contusions that crawled over all my body and my mind. What was going on? What were these voices in my head, this crying, this wailing, this screaming, this sobbing? How could I one moment be pleasantly bobbing along, lost in my work, and the very next I am a blur of unabridged distress? These thoughts—where did they come from? These feelings? These urges, that aren't *my urges?* These compulsions? These random, illogical needs? They feel as if they are not coming from *me*, as if they don't belong to *me*. Am I mad? No, I'm not mad: I'm traumatised. This is what trauma does to you— separating you off from yourself, from your experiences, from your now-world. And a trigger—a present-day reminder in some tiny, inconsequential way in the here-and-now environment—connects you again to that trauma. That's not madness. That's the beginnings of sanity.

Sometimes the triggers are overwhelming and I switch to another part. But mostly they just barge into my consciousness, unwelcome guests dragging with them a house-party of traumatised feelings and knowledge and perceptions. Switching is easy. Intrusions are not. Switching is a release clause, a checking-out when it's all too much; life is much harder with this constant tumult of dissociative voices, but without the escape. It's exhausting. Am I the me who is calm and objective and competent? Or am I the me who is jumpy and hyperalert, barraged by the irritable, paranoid warnings of a traumatised self? To that part of me, *everything* speaks danger; *everything* speaks threat. They see the world through a filter of unrepressed hostility. And I can feel that worldview within myself, but it is not *my* worldview. Trauma has given them that worldview. I was not traumatised, so I don't feel so wary. Both mindsets exist within me simultaneously— that is what 'multiple' means to me.

But I've had six brutal years now of working through the trauma, working on me connecting again to these others parts of myself, working on empathising *with myself* and having compassion *on myself* and making connections and a thousand 'Aha!' moments of understanding *so that's why I do that*—and I have squirmed with the reluctance of accepting that I have parts and parts who have suffered as they have. I've come to understand why the dissociative barriers have been there: conflicts so huge that no mind could hold them all together in one place at one time. I have DID because of those conflicts: for me the central one is *I am strong and I will survive and it is shameful to be trampled on* versus the barefaced reality of *I am weak and I may not survive and I am constantly being trampled on.* There are others: *I love them* and *I hate them; I need them* and *they hurt me; I like this and I hate this; I have to deal with this* and *there's no good way to deal with this.*

But six years on and the barriers have thinned. I am not egg-boxed in any more, sound-proofed and feeling-proofed against the other parts of myself that I had to dissociate from to survive. So now, after switching, when I'm back, there isn't the ink-black void there used to be. Sometimes when I'm gone, I'm there on the back row, watching warily, unable to intervene, unable to *know* even what I'm going to do next. But there's a link, a connection, a sense that I'm in the same brain-universe, in the same here-now context as this other part of myself. Or even when I'm not, when there's no co-consciousness, there is a sense afterwards like of dreaming: it's there, on the tip of my tongue, on the tip of my mind, the shadowy-surreal sense of what's just gone on. If I strain, I can remember it.

Mostly, though, I don't want to strain; I still don't want to know most of it. It will be painful, and life clamours all around me with the responsibilities of adulthood: I haven't got time, right here, right now, to feel that pain. I haven't got space, right here, right now, with a real-life teenage foster daughter pouting in a real-life *my-phone-credit-ran-out* strop, right here, right now. There isn't the capacity on the inside of me, with everything pulled taut with trauma and the exhaustion of *going there,* for me to feel this right now. So I don't look, I don't strain to see into the dreamworld that is my other selves, and I put it on the shelf until later. I've come to appreciate my need to be able to manage 'normal' life, the here-and-now life of work and adult responsibilities and family life, and I appreciate these dissociative barriers that allow me to do that. But I've also been building doorways into the barriers so that I can come and go as I need to.

Sometimes, I don't know and I can't know what has gone on in a switch, but it leaks back to me later, like icemelt in my mind. I call this 'post-consciousness': the knowing afterwards, when there is air in my lungs and looseness in my muscles, when I've got the capacity to know. When I can breathe, I want to know. I want to connect with these other parts of myself, these guardians and recipients of the *too-much* that I endured as a child. Their pain now is still *too-much* but it's not spitting any more, like water in hot fat: the temperature has been turned down. There's more control. Not as much as I'd like, not as much as I need, but it's not the emotional chip-pan fire it used to be. The more I've got in touch with my parts, the less they intrude uninvited into daily life. There is a place for my trauma to come out and be heard, and that's in therapy. Six years has taught me that that's a safe place, that it's a big place, with sturdy, strong walls that can absorb my combustion. It hasn't burst into flames with the ferocity of my suffering. And six years has taught me that it will be there next week too, that I can wait that long, that although there might not be enough time next week, there'll be more time the week after that, and we're not going to run out of time in the end. I can have feelings, I can have big, difficult, skin-shredding emotions and they won't destroy me and there *is* such a thing as soothing. There *is* a way to calm down. I can feel big feelings *because* they won't destroy me. They keep trying, but they haven't succeeded. They're not scaring me so much anymore.

Life with dissociation isn't easy. But life wouldn't even *be* without dissociation, so I'm grateful for it. Slowly the links are being made between the different parts of me, and the different parts of my experience. It gets harder, in a way, the less I switch: I am more conscious of what previously was cut off from me. Knowledge, feelings, urges leak through from the inside parts of me. They are not always welcome; they are not always convenient. But they are all part of the bigger experience of *me-being-me* that I am striving for through therapy. The more I accept my dissociated experiences, the less they intrude. But they do still intrude, and a lot of the time now I know about it too. 'Getting better' doesn't always mean 'getting easier,' at least not to start with. But the alternative is to remain dissociative for the rest of my life, cut off from parts of me that are, intrinsically, *me*. And that's just not an option.

CHAPTER EIGHT

Shame

If I had to choose one single characteristic of someone with DID, who has suffered serious abuse, what would it be? Their dissociation? The presence of alters? Their post-traumatic symptoms such as flashbacks and hypervigilance? Actually, for me, I would say that the thread that marks us all, that is the ubiquitous watermark in the story of all our lives, is shame. A few years ago, in a flash of insight about how drenched in shame my life has been, I wrote this in my journal:

> I would do anything not to be me. And that, in effect, is what I have done, by being DID. I have become a shifting multitude of other people, other parts, other personalities. Anything, anything, but me. That is the restless sense I have now every day—of trying to get away from myself, of trying to twizzle away from the reality of me-being-me, to keep my mind busy and alert and active on a range of things, on anything, but not on the awareness of me-being-me. I know—I know—deep down I know that these things are true and that these things happened and that try as I might to distance myself from them, to push them into ego-alien memory fragments and alter personalities, they are—they always will be—me. It is me, me, me: the me who was hurt and abused and taken as a baby, as an infant, as a child, and used for other people's evil and malice. My self-concept is thus imprisoned in the wrongness of being me.

Shame is a strange thing. We can feel so ashamed of feeling ashamed that it can be hard even to think about it, to talk about it. How many times, when we've dared to allude to it, when we've allowed it to poke its head just a millimetre above the parapet, when we've tried to talk about this most disabling of feelings, has someone responded: 'Oh you've got nothing to be ashamed of!' And then down it bobs and scuttles away in shame… 'I'm ashamed for feeling ashamed.'

Guilt is so much easier to deal with. Guilt says, 'I did something bad,' and that can be fixed, that can be put right, we can pay for it or maybe even die for it, and there's a clear transaction that needs to take place. Of course many of us struggle with guilt too, that caving-in feeling inside when we know we've done wrong and we accept the bad feelings it gives to us. But shame is more insidious. It's not about what we did wrong. It's about us being wrong, just because we are. It's a core organising principle of our psyche, our identity and view of ourselves—'This is who I am.' Like a weed, it wraps itself around our entire system of selves, strangling our relationships, our good feelings, our experiences, our hopes. It can smother us to death.

And we all have a phobia of shame—we would do almost anything not to feel shame: it burns and scalds like bleach in our entrails. So we avoid shame unconsciously, before we even know we have, because it's such a potent, repulsive thing. But in our minds, we know it's there and it shows up in our self-talk and the background dribble of our thoughts: I am ashamed of who I am. I am stupid, I'm incompetent, I'm pathetic, I'm inept, I'm disgusting, I'm crazy, I'm bad. Everything I want, everything I think, everything I feel, everything I do is shameful and toxic.

And it can be so constant, like motorway hum, that we only recognise its presence when we can get away, find a sunny patch of meadow miles from the screech of tyres and the grind of engines, and listen to the silence. Shame was so normal for me that I had to experience those moments of silence—those moments of 'unshame'— before I could consider the new paradigm of living without shame roaring unnoticed in my ears.

And I had to realise that shame has its purpose. Some say that lies in evolutionary biology, that we had our best chance of survival in group, where we could pool our resources, find a mate, share childcare, defend against predators. So if belonging to a group was good news, then we needed an inbuilt instinct—shame—to warn us of behaviours that might threaten our place in that group. And each 'group' has its own rules—like the teenagers in secondary school who are 'in' when they wear their tie upside down or their shirt hanging out; the football supporters with their replica kits, their chants, their insistence that 4-4-2 is the only proper way to play; even the therapists, with their purple or beige cardigans and membership of BACP. When we contravene the 'rules,' we are shamed, and the purpose of the hardwiring of our response is to redirect our actions to what the group finds acceptable, because rejection risks death.

But what if the group itself is dysfunctional? What if we live in a society that elevates celebrity and power and success? What if the brutal survival instinct of that group means that only the fittest are 'in' and the lost and lonely, the depressed and the abused, the shy and the faltering, the mentally ill, are thrown to the wolves? We feel so 'faulty'—we have panic attacks and lose time, we are triggered and have flashbacks, we cope with compulsive behaviours around food and sex and alcohol and drugs, our emotions are like a snowstorm, our relationships beset with struggles—and the rules of the group tell us that we are wrong to be distressed, that our reactions are bizarre, that it is more important to 'act normal' than it is to deal with our trauma, and that we should hide or deny or suppress what has happened to us. And the shame from that is an agony of daily reality for many of us. I sometimes think that the only way to be acceptable in normal society is for me to shed 95% of who and what I am. If I could just excise this trauma from my life, the way it has changed me and shaped me—for good and for bad—then maybe I could join in with the vacuous inanity of Britain's Got Talent without the feeling that I'm a fraud and a squatter.

Society then doesn't generally want you to speak out about your symptoms, your life, your struggles. There is the shame of being silenced—and no-one really wants you to talk about your history or your abuse either. It's a hush-hush thing. The lack of treatment options on the NHS then suggests that you're not worth helping or you're being a nuisance or you're too damaged to treat, or to be worth treating. After all, isn't it better for the group as a whole if we throw a few weaklings to assuage the wolves' hunger? Then if you tell people about being dissociative or having been abused, people shrink back. Imperceptibly perhaps, but they do shrink back. So the core message we hear is an intrinsically shaming one: 'Shut up and be quiet and don't bother us with your nasty abuse histories and your mental illnesses!'

This society we live in values 'stuff' more than people. It values perfection and success, not the limp and struggle of the misfits: the lost, the lonely, the depressed or the abused. We know we don't measure up to the standards around us, and we know we never can, however much the adverts scream at us that we 'deserve' a new kitchen that we simply cannot afford. We are basically 'out' and there's nothing we can do to get back 'in,' and the shame of that runs deep. Of course, it's society that ought to be ashamed of itself, not us—but how often do the perpetrators feel the shame they ought to? They shift that onto us, and we take it because we've never known another way.

But I wasn't born with this shame. It's not my lot in life. It helped me enormously to realise that it is the experiences that I've had that have nurtured this shame in me, but it's not my birthright. And if it's experiences that grew it, then new experiences can shrink it too.

One of the core developmental roots of shame is our unmet needs in childhood. If we don't receive the care and nurture and love that as infants we need, we develop a sense of self that we are unworthy of care: that we are 'bad.' Not that we have done something bad, but that we are bad, intrinsically. Our shame-based identity may then be reinforced by the implicit or explicit messages that we received in the home or during the abuse: 'You're no good,' 'You're a waste of space,' 'You're useless,' 'You're ugly,' 'You're pathetic.' And so often we take these voices into ourselves, and in DID they may became the critical parts of our self that pick at us all day telling us that we can't: we can't succeed, we can't be loved, we can't be liked, we can't be clever. And in some of us they evolve into actual alters—our 'introjected perpetrator' parts whose mindset is modelled on our abusers, who repeat what they have heard, reflecting our abusers' antipathy and disgust.

That's when shame is reinforced by shame. Our core sense of badness is reinforced by ourselves, by our parts which replay the abusive scripts of our past even though we may be miles and decades away from those original voices. When our persecutory alters then act out, and harm us or threaten others, when their shame-driven fury erupts into real life with all its consequences and hardcore limits, then shame swallows us again, that we've got these so-called 'bad' parts of us who are doing 'bad' things which then proves and reinforces our supposed 'badness.' It's a self-fulfilling prophecy.

For those of us with a dissociative disorder who were sexually abused in childhood, the shame of nakedness and violation, of our privacy being not just invaded but obliterated, is crippling—a total flood of overwhelming and uncopeable feelings. Somehow we inculcate the accusation of being 'damaged goods': a broken, dirty, good-for-nothing doll discarded in a skip. We've been dirtied by the abuse and the feeling screams inside that no-one will want to cuddle us or cherish us ever again. This deep, Stig-of-the-dump conviction infiltrates our intimate relationships and we believe we must be deceiving this poor husband or wife or partner or friend or therapist that they would want to have anything to do with us: we are slap-bang up against this core belief that we are good-for-nothing, broken beyond repair. And it's an active agent within us, because of our sense that we are toxic, and we will infect them if they get too close. I wrote this in my journal several years ago:

> I'm feeling angry or something now as I write this. It's like a stirred-up agitation inside, and I want to damage something. What do I want to damage? My abusers? No, no, that would be wrong, bad, too dangerous. I want to damage MYSELF. I want to go out and drive my car really fast, really dangerously, push it to the limit and slam it headlong into a tree. I HATE FEELING LIKE THIS. I FEEL SO WRONG INSIDE, so malformed or something, like intrinsically toxic and shameful and bad, all broken and rusting and twisted, decayed, spewing filth and vomit and in need of TOTAL DESTRUCTION. A core of absolute filth, mustn't touch it, mustn't see it, mustn't go anywhere near it, like some poisonous radioactive scum that will destroy everything around it.

I blamed myself for the abuse—for wanting the relationship with the people who groomed me, as if I had poisoned them and they wouldn't have abused me but for my own toxicity. It's never a child's fault, but shame clouded every thought and attempt by me to believe otherwise. And enjoyment, or pleasure, or desire, or laughter: the presence of any of these in my memory, alongside the abuse, alongside the relationship that led to the abuse, decried my innocence. The shame of it burned hotly. How could I enjoy being with someone who abused me? But I did, and it's normal, and it's because abuse occurs in a matrix of trickery and grooming and manipulation and deceit, and we are led blindfold into a pit and then blamed by the abuser for dragging them there as well.

When memories of abuse flood back, in these dissociated fragments of somatosensory experience, the shame floods right back in as well— the shame we felt during the abuse, the degrading, humiliating acts we were forced to endure or perform, the powerlessness, the shame of exploited vulnerability. Sexual abuse is always wrong and damaging, but in ritual abuse there is a degree of intentional humiliation and degradation that has as its motivation only the sadistic desire to crush the child to a nothing and to eviscerate their soul. The shame we feel now—at being abused, at knowing our abusers, at our family history or family connections that invited or colluded with the abuse—is compounded by these body flashbacks of the shame that we felt then. In our disclosures, in processing the trauma, shame is the puppet-master behind us, limiting our moves, directing our flight into the avoidance of downcast eyes and cowering withdrawal, the silent contortions of not having words to express it, not having feelings to feel it. We need to keep the therapist at a distance and not contaminate them with this thick, black, tar-like yuck of shame that we seem to breed from within ourselves. In remembering and processing and moving beyond the shame, it's a constant struggle with shame to be able to go there at all.

For many survivors, certainly for me, the shame of forced perpetration is the final taboo. The very memories of it are layered under thick, gloopy shame, dissociated away because they are too painful to contemplate. And perhaps it's because of our innate sense of good and bad, our biological drive to be part of the 'group', and the knowledge that in our society, a 'paedophile'—a 'pervert' or 'monster' as the tabloids would label them—is the most depraved form of life. The angry, vicious, hateful mob baying for blood outside Court when the likes of Ian Huntley or Vanessa George are sentenced is the hatred we fear. When we have been forced to sexually abuse, or physically abuse, or maim or even murder another child, maybe even a baby, then we feel only the shame and vile disgust of the societal anger and fear directed against us. As a child, we can't see it for what it is—a choiceless choice, an abuse of our will, unutterable duress. We just feel that the act defines our identity: that now we are an abuser too. So everything that we hate and fear about our own abusers, we turn back on ourselves. We become a lightning rod for all the outrage and all the hurt that we feel for what was done to us—it loops around and lands squarely back on us because now we are the perpetrator. That's why we hate ourselves so much, why we feel so ashamed. We live with the constant fear of exposure: we live with the anxious hiccupping expectation that once you know, we won't know you anymore.

Shame can also be a defence. This is obvious when you think about it, but I never cease to amaze myself by how many difficult things I just don't think about: dissociation is a way of thought. But it's blindingly self-evident: either I am bad, or my abusers are. And it's always easier to blame yourself than it is to blame your attachment figures. It is intolerable to think of them as 'bad'—that makes the world too scary, and there is nothing that you can do about it. If you are bad, then at least you can have some control over your own badness: you can try to be good; you can punish yourself. John Briere sums this up neatly in what he calls the 'Abuse Dichotomy' in his book Child Abuse Trauma (1992):

> I am being hurt, emotionally or physically, by a parent or other adult whom I love, care for, and trust deeply. Based on how I think about the world thus far, this injury can only be due to one of two things: either I am bad, or my parent is bad. But I have been taught by other adults, either at home or at school, that parents are always right, and always do things for my own good (any alternative is simply too frightening). So when parents or carers occasionally hurt me, it is for my own good, because I have been bad. This is called punishment. Therefore, it must be my fault that I am being hurt, just as my parent says. This must be

punishment. I must deserve this. Therefore, I am as bad as whatever is done to me. The punishment must fit the crime: anything else suggests my parents are bad, which I have rejected because my parents do things for my own good. I am bad because I have been hurt. I have been hurt because I am bad. But I am hurt quite often, and/or quite deeply. Therefore I must be very bad.

Placing the badness in the abuser rather than the abused is often the hardest part of our recovery. I wish it were easier; I wish this infection of shame would clear with a single course of therapy-antibiotics. I wish the people who ought to feel ashamed would stop blame-shifting. With consummate skill they slide it sideways into our laps, like a conjuring card trick, so that we take the punishment for their shameful acts, and they can stare shamelessly into the camera and harrumph loudly at these 'spiteful and totally false' allegations that we are making. I wish their lies didn't mess with our heads so easily, that a single denial causes us to twirl around within ourselves wondering if we've made it all up. But instead we live these shame-constricted lives, where shame is truer than truth, and where therapy is our only option for relief.

But shame doesn't just lead us to the therapy room; shame manifests in the therapy room as a result of the therapy itself. The fundamental vulnerability of needing therapy at all is further increased by this strange, alien environment, with a therapist who has been to 'therapy school' to learn the rules and create this break-from-reality headspace: we don't understand the rules, at least not at first, and they have the power and we don't. And that in itself is a reminder of our traumatic powerlessness and evokes continual ripples of shame, as we struggle to answer the questions, and struggle to contain our neediness, and struggle—shamefully, oh so shamefully—to come to terms with the past that we deny and all these shameful, rejected, disowned parts of our self with their attachment needs grinding mercilessly away at our adult avoidance. I wrote this in my journal a few years ago:

I hide too well. I don't want to show anyone my real self, all riddled with doubt and self-hatred and this whining, incessantly needy child inside, brattish, spoilt, vacuous, pathetic. I hate my needy parts. They are wrong, wrong, wrong—so wrong. Neediness is shameful—whacked out of you, taunted, demeaned. It's the nastiness of a caregiver offering comfort and solace and then humiliatingly scoffing and mocking that you said you wanted it: pathetic child. I felt so hated. There was nothing my abusers hated about me more than neediness, cringeing, whining, wanting, crying. *Shut your mouth. Pack it in. Stop that awful noise. Pull yourself together. Grow up. Don't you dare cry.*

Effective therapy by its very nature takes you to a deeply vulnerable place where your innermost needs are exposed. If you had the kind of childhood environment that I did and that is so common amongst DID survivors, having needs was shameful and it was actively shamed. Those feelings are then re-elicited within the therapeutic relationship, so in working through the shame, shame looms large. It's shameful to want, need, and wish; it's shameful to feel weak, and vulnerable, and alone; it's shameful to struggle, it's shameful to feel, it's shameful to do everything that happens in therapy. No wonder the whole thing feels so excruciatingly like a trick.

Shames causes us to hide and isolate. We avoid people. We put on a 'false self' to people. We keep ourselves to ourselves—we don't go out, we run away from relationships, from interaction with people. But in DID we don't just put on one 'false self,' we take on a whole stack of alternate personalities. I believe that the creation or at least the maintenance of alter personalities is not just based in trauma and dissociation, but is also driven by shame. The essence of DID is about not wanting to be me: the me that was abused, the me that is so needy and dependent and pathetic now. So we alienate and compartmentalise the shadow sides of our selves, and push them or exile them into alternate personalities. We can't deny our attachment needs, but we can push them away from our competent, adult selves into our 'little ones,' who can more safely express them. Or we have angry and hostile parts of our selves. But having been taught that anger is wrong or bad, we are ashamed of it—so we squeeze it out from our good-girl exterior into disowned parts of the self. And it's the same with self-harm or comfort-eating or any other form of medicating pain away—we allow the shame of that to sit with 'someone else,' another part of us who can be safely blamed from a distance, keeping the adult self safely ensconced away from such 'unacceptable' practices. And aside from the purpose of self-harm to reduce pain rather than to cause it, there is also a shame-based form in which we act out our hatred against the self for being so toxic and bad. And then the scars shame us further.

To deal with shame, we also compensate. In response to feeling so bad, we excel at being good. We're the nicest person in the world; the most helpful; the most loving; the most caring; the most patient; the most compliant; the most hardworking. So many of us with DID have ended up in the caring professions and much of that I suspect is driven by us compensating for the sense of shame and badness that we feel by 'loving' others—either to make up for how bad we really are on the inside, or to cover it over so that no-one will see it, and reject us. Of course in reality we are a motley bunch, just as loving or unloving as other people. Dare to reject our 'love' and 'care,' however, and we'll show you how spiteful we can be! But we push all our nastiness into invisible parts and beam broadly out of our niceness to the world around us. And then we are tormented by the knowledge that hidden inside us, lurking there in secret shame, is a part called Destroyer or Evil One or (in my case) Dark. Of course 'Dark' doesn't really belong to me, so that means that I'm Always Nice. It was a nice theory, while it lasted. Progress in therapy for me has seen a paradoxical increase in my 'nastiness'—less of the good girl, more of the 'this is real' girl, less of the extremes of Dark's pent-up explosions, more of a mix of the nice and the nasty in the outward me, who has also learned to say no.

Dark's malice is obvious, but self-sabotage is much harder to spot. It's not as conscious or as deliberate as self-harm, but it's every bit as damaging. It's the way that we do things at an unconscious level to trip ourselves up, or to prove to people that we really are bad and useless and shouldn't be trusted. We don't let ourselves succeed. Shame tells us that we don't deserve it. Just as we're approaching some new height of relationship, or career, or therapeutic breakthrough—we blast a hole in our balloon, and plummet back to earth. So often, we are at our most dangerous when we are at our most successful. We glimpse the 'good,' and that contradicts our built-in, shame-based belief system of self-evident badness and toxicity, and so we react suddenly to restore the status quo. A therapist's compliment comes with a misinterpreted message: 'Watch out, watch out, there's danger about!' It's just too contradictory to our shame-based identity to be able to absorb a compliment as a safe and positive thing, so we balance it up by hearing it as a threat, a prelude to abuse.

But there is hope. There is a cure. Shame will tell us that there is none, and that we don't deserve one anyway, but in Phil Mollon's words, the cure for shame is empathy. Shame disconnects us from people—it puts us, as we've seen, outside the group, excluded and unwanted. Empathy, on the other hand, reconnects us to people. It puts us on the same wavelength, looking eyeball-to-eyeball, experiencing the other's experience and being in the same psychological living space. Empathy restores to us the hope that we can be part of the group. Reconnecting with an other, we smell the scent of possibility, that if one might accept us, then maybe the group might too. An attuned, human relationship is key. That's what we're looking for, and that's what is so effective in therapy.

But most people are so averse to the emotional experience of shame, because it is so uncomfortable and distressing, that they stay at a distance, misattuned and remote, and say, 'Don't be ashamed.' But how hard is it to reach down into someone's shame-filled existence and sit there for a while with them in it, to breathe it in, to get to know the colour and the hue of this shame, to taste it, to feel it under your fingers? Just by doing that—by attuning and sitting closely by—the shame starts to recede. But shame never obeys the command given from a distance to leave. Shame is the experience of being outside the camp. You've got to come outside the camp to reach me and make the camp come this far, to extend its boundaries—then there will be no shame, when I know that I am as human as you are, because you have got that close to me for me to smell what unshame smells like.

This is the power that a therapist has with their client—to offer that opportunity to safely reconnect to another person and not be rejected. If we can make that connection, we will start to see shame shift. And partners can do it, and friends, and supporters too—the key is being an attuned human being, not your job description.

Shame is a central experience of being a dissociative survivor of trauma. It infects and controls so much of what we do. We are ashamed to talk about shame. We are ashamed to challenge it. We are ashamed to need the attuned human relationship that we know will cure it, because we fear that no-one will want to give it to us. And so perhaps the first step in overcoming shame is in our accepting ourselves. For those of us with DID, that means accepting all the parts of our self, however shameful, however angry, however badly behaved or persecutory or malicious. It means realising that we have disowned what we cannot bear and we have forced it into the recesses. But it's still there. We have good reason to be the way that we are, and most of us want to change. But shaming ourselves for being the way we are is the worst way to facilitate that change. Shame breeds shame. I have found, and I am still finding, that empathy is indeed the cure for shame, and I need it not just from others, but from myself towards my selves as well. As I develop that empathy, as I allow the soft 'ouch' of compassion to replace the hardened abuse of my inner voices, shame is starting to shift. I've got a long way to go, but I'm no longer ashamed of how far.

CHAPTER NINE

Rediscovering Eden

The pain, every month, had always been terrible since my periods had begun, 24 years earlier. Sometimes unbearable to the point of passing out, reluctantly, desperately, I underwent diagnostic medical procedures to try to identify a cause. Endometriosis, fibroids, pelvic inflammatory disease: whatever was suspected was declared, after laparoscopic investigation, not guilty. There was nothing 'wrong' inside, no physical reason for the pain, and no explanation either for the subfertility that had resulted in only 3 conceptions in over 7 years of attempts at pregnancy, all of which had resulted in miscarriage.

All of this, though, was merely a backdrop to twice-weekly psychotherapy in which I was disclosing, with reckless celerity, my dissociated history of ritual abuse. The therapist plea to 'slow down' was met by me with incredulity and bewilderment: how could it possibly be better to 'vomit slowly,' as I put it? I wanted to get it out, out from the cloistered, clammy confines of my unconscious, out from the musty injunctions of 'Tell no-one,' and out into the free, fresh light where I could see that my experiences had affected me, but were not me. It was a severe, torturous time. Memories came through the body first—pain, unbelievable, scream-aloud pain, and nausea, tastes, feelings, coldness, shock. For over two years the narrative, barely narratable, tumbled out, senseless and shocking and freshly traumatic. Was it the right thing to do? Was I being retraumatised by the telling? Did we have to go through this awful nightmare of disclosure? But how could we not?—inside me, I was driven by a desperation no longer to be alone with my secrets, and gripped by a belief that once 'out,' once named, I could own it and face it and stare it down, and I would not be so controlled by it any more: I could overcome it. 'They are only memories,' we would say grimly to our therapist, and she would echo grimly back, 'It's not happening now.'

Then November. Somehow we made it through the triggers and compulsions, the 'programs' and reminders of Halloween. But, despite expecting things to pick up, somehow they worsened. Words in journals, pictures and diagrams, rapid-switch turn-taking for alters: something was brewing, but with an intolerable air around it, of places in our mind we did not want to go, of pain too huge to bear. The body began to tell the story: heart-pounding terror, sleepless dread, and pain like menstrual cramps, only stronger, more insistent—pain that came in waves. First one alter and then another began to disclose fragments of their story. The jigsaw began to come together.

It was a house with a red door, a big house on the High Street of a village near where we lived when we were growing up. Did it used to be a doctors' surgery? We couldn't remember. A big house, a red door in the middle. Inside there were high ceilings and panelled walls. We were in a room, it was dark, a dim kind of light, an empty-ish room with a bed or something against the wall, with a door off to the right of the bed. There are hushed voices, light through the door, people coming and going, but we don't know who they are. There is a girl, she is 12 or 13, she is on the bed, we are watching her; the girl is us.

And pain. Waves and waves of belly-gripping, burning pain, and terror because we think we are going to die, it hurts so much. And this goes on for hours. People come and stick something long and thin and pointy up us, explain the alters. There is pain, and more pain, and pain, and more pain. On and on for hours, mostly us left alone, terrified and terrorised, on this bed and in this room. We can't remember who brought us there, we can't remember why. Just people coming and going, low voices, low light, and pain.

Then at last there is blood and they are pleased, and there is a baby. I give birth to a baby. I give birth to a baby. I see this baby, tiny and bloodied, but alive, and I see them take the baby out of the room.

They take her out of the room, towards the light, and everyone leaves and I am alone. And I wait. Other things happened, I'm sure, but all I remember is that I wait. I wait for them to bring back my baby. Why don't I move? Why don't I get up and go and look for her? Why don't I do something? But nothing. I do nothing and all I am left with is the sight of my bloodied little baby as they took her away, and never bring her back. I don't remember a cry. I don't remember going home. I don't remember anything else.

Now, in November, in therapy, I begin to see what I know to be true: that was me on the bed; that was my baby. Conceived from rape, born in secrecy, killed: my baby.

The realisation of this event hit me hard. I tried but failed to dismiss it as untrue. I knew it to be true; I had always known it, I had just never let myself know it. It fitted. It hurt.

I had had this terrible, disabling period pain every month for as long as I could remember, but in December it was different. And January, and February... It was still painful, but nothing like previously. And the entirety of my adult life had been a seeking to put right what had been wrong: I fostered 22 children, mostly babies—I loved them, cared for them, was hugely attentive to them. In my dreams was a constant searching for a baby, or finding a baby dead but not alive. Suddenly the pieces dropped into place.

How did I deal with it in therapy? Of crucial importance to me was the fact that my baby was a real person, and I couldn't bear for her to be so secretive, so unknown. She was a real, live person who would have grown up to be a real, live person like me or you, and yet she was born and she died in utmost secrecy, without a name even.

I knew that she was a girl; I couldn't remember specifically knowing why, but eventually I just knew. So the first thing I did was to name her. This was painful: how do you find a name for a dead baby, for a daughter you will never have? I looked in baby name books with a sick feeling in my stomach. At last I called her Eden, the name evocative for me of God's original intention in the garden: of His love, perfection and beauty. But it gave her a sense of reality too: here was a real baby, with a real name—my baby.

Grief overwhelmed me, suddenly and unexpectedly. Like the 'frozen peas' analogy where the emotions came out as fresh as the day they were frozen, it was like stepping back in time, as if it had only just happened. I felt shock, pain, upset; numb, angry, listless; sad—feelings revolved and revolved as if I were at the centre of a maelstrom. But it was good to feel, however 'bad' the feelings. I went to church, having told no-one except my therapist and my husband, and I remember wanting to stop the service and shout: 'Don't you realise what's happened? Don't you realise that my baby is dead?' I felt trapped into silence, and yet betrayed by the secret, as if I were betraying Eden by keeping quiet. This was a human being, created in the image of God, with all the dignity of a human being, and yet no-one knew her, no-one had ever even heard about her, and no-one cared or did anything about her murder. I was in emotional turmoil with the most appalling, painful grief, and yet at church and amongst friends I felt enforced into silence. Why? Because they wouldn't cope? It felt as if I were pushing things too far to expect ordinary people to hear about a child giving birth to a baby after rape, and the baby being killed. But that did nothing of course to ease my isolation, or process my grief.

In therapy I began to think in terms of what I would do if the circumstances were more 'normal.' What would I do if I had been pregnant by my husband and the baby had been stillborn or had died shortly after birth? I needed a vehicle for my grief.

Naming Eden was an important first step. I then decided to gather together a 'memory box' for her. This felt cruel in its irony—over 20 years of traumagenic amnesia and then no 'special memories' to recall anyway. I read about what other parents did in 'normal' stillbirth or similar circumstances: locks of hair, photographs, the babygrow, the hospital wrist-tag, a funeral. None of these were either practicable or possible. The frustration of powerlessness then: the inability to do anything to grieve.

So I decided on a new kind of 'memory box'—a 'what if' memory box. Trawling the internet I found a beautiful, customised white box with lilac gingham trim and Eden's name. And I began to fill it with objects that I would have bought for her. On a trip into Mothercare I felt overwhelmed with furious, impotent pain: IT'S NOT FAIR. I was terrified in case a store assistant asked me who the blanket was for, and more terrified in case I saw someone who knew me. I would have been incapable of restraining an angry, inappropriate retort: 'It's for my dead baby.'

A blanket from Mothercare, a book from Amazon, a soft toy from John Lewis, a card from Clinton's. Then a babygrow in 'Very Premature' size, which felt doll-like tiny and yet almost too large. Every item was placed carefully but ragefully in the box—'It doesn't bring her back!' No, but it allowed me to be upset, to feel what I was feeling, to express those feelings, to provide a focus. I was determined not to dissociate-away my feelings this time. It was okay for me to feel, even the 'bad' feelings.

But I needed something more personal, something more unique than mass-produced consumer items. Through pain, even tears, I emailed a long-standing friend who knew a little, a very very little, of my background, and who had made my wedding dress for me. I told her, straightforwardly, about Eden, not dodging the truth, not shamefully hiding Eden away as a bad secret. What else could I do and still ask for what I wanted? I wanted her to make Eden a quilt.

My friend had done this before for one of the babies I had fostered, and the quilt went with the child into her adoptive family. That was what I wanted for Eden—something that said 'Eden,' and was real, and was for her, her alone. I asked for a very small quilt, because my memory of Eden was that she was very, very small.

A few weeks later, the quilt arrived. I cried; it was so beautiful, and Eden was so real. Most days I couldn't bear to look at her memory box. I still couldn't understand why the world didn't seem to notice: it engulfed me, while the people around were blissfully, cruelly unaware. It was the loneliness of a secret, and a secret injustice. The world watched X-Factor and Strictly Come Dancing, and I ached for the baby I had never been able to hold, the baby I felt I had failed.

There were other factors to process: what did this event 'mean'? Who had known about it? How could a 12- or 13-year-old girl be pregnant and no-one know? I traced back my history: here was an explanation for the weeks off school I missed, the end-of-year exams

I had had to take later than everyone else, sat alone in the school library. The collusion, after the event, seemed obvious. But at the time, as a child, as a dissociative child, it was all I knew — it was all I didn't know.

Other connections began to be made: my inordinate terror of doctors and all medical procedures, things that alters had been saying, in bits and pieces, for years in therapy. Memories burst like bubbles: more acts of the perpetrators at the time, the family context, the sense I had unconsciously made of it. In therapy we worked on my false guilt, the frozenness of trauma that had meant that I didn't move, and the endless, craving seeking for my baby. On one particularly distressed day, one of my alters drove us to find the house with the big red door. It was there, dusty and aged, but otherwise just as we remembered it. The alter, confused in a time-warp, went to see if our baby was there. But there was no answer at the door and of course no baby: 23 years have passed at least. Eden may even have been a mother herself by now.

What do I make of 'motherhood' with my own mother infanticidally oriented first to me and then, in actual reality of completed deed, towards my own baby? What is a mother? I have been a long-term foster mother, struggling with the issue of 'contact' between our foster daughter and her own abusive birth mother, who left her with head injuries as a 6-month-old baby. How do I define a 'mother'? What do I do with my inability to carry a baby to term within my own body, with the fears of what kind of mother I too might become, fears unfounded but viscerally held?

I would like to wrap this up neatly, three steps and we are free and there is no more pain or grief or doubting or denial or despair. Sometimes it seems that the trauma is so great that we need some wipe-clean magic to cope with it. But that only serves to avoid the pain for longer. It doesn't bring Eden back from the dead or cause my mother to love me. Is it the truth that sets me free? What is that truth?

For me, it is partly that Eden is dead and I am not a mother.

Long live Eden.

CHAPTER TEN

Ten steps towards recovery

Two timelines characterise my life: before my 'breakdown' and after it. Almost out of the blue, on a sunny day in April 2005, my life changed forever and the dissociative walls and barriers which had held my trauma at bay for 32 years suddenly collapsed. It heralded the arrival of flashbacks, body memories and the appearance of dozens of separate parts of my personality. Life has never been the same since. But in those early days and months, I had no guidebook for what was ahead, no route marked out on a map for me. Someone recently asked me what I would say to myself, the 'me' of eight years ago. What would I tell myself of what is ahead and what advice would I give?

This chapter is my attempt to answer that question. I believe passionately in recovery from dissociative identity disorder: not because I am 'recovered,' as if that exists as some finite point of reality, but because I have been moving towards recovery for the last eight years. DID is perfectly logical: a creative way of surviving otherwise unendurable trauma. And the brain that learned to cope using dissociation can now learn to cope using other strategies: our brains are 'plastic' and geared towards new learning. My life is very different now from the first few years after my breakdown. And there are ten things that I wish I could say to that newly-dissociative me — ten things which I have found invaluable in making the journey from eight years ago to where I am today and which I am sure will all continue to guide me for a great many years to come too.

1. Find a therapist

It took me over a year to find a therapist. In those first thirteen months, I exhausted my narrow friendship circle and I nearly lost my marriage because I didn't understand what was going on and nor did anyone around me. The weight of trauma that causes DID cannot be carried alone and nor can it be carried by well-meaning friends. Therapy is a safe place to bring and process my trauma. It is a safe place to bring and explore the dissociative parts of my personality. It is a safe place to bring and explore the templates for relationship that I have grown up with.

Dissociative disorders are caused by trauma and so recovery must at some level involve dealing with that in order to move beyond it. The 'symptoms,' the experiences we have in our dissociative lives — the flashbacks, the body memories, the emotional ups-and-downs that we cope with through self-harm or addictions or numbing, the switching, the amnesia, the voices, the denial, the distress — they are not a normal, 'ideal' way to live. I want to resolve my 'symptoms,' resolve the trauma that had given rise to those symptoms, and learn how to live. All the self-will in the world hadn't got me to that point before I started therapy. I needed someone else to stand outside of me and help me see what is true and what is only perception. Long-term, un-pressured, un-rushed, without-agenda therapy has been the single most helpful thing on my road towards recovery. I just wish I had started it sooner.

2. Education, education, education

The biggest obstacle to me getting help eight years ago was my total ignorance of mental health. I didn't even know what counselling was. But as I began to read and investigate, the confusion of what was happening to me began to clear. Once I'd been introduced to dissociation, I began to realise that DID is an entirely logical response to trauma. Once I realised that dissociative disorders were on a spectrum with post traumatic stress disorder (PTSD), they began to seem more mainstream. Once I started to understand that the dissociative parts of the personality have a function and a meaning, I began to see how I had survived trauma by compartmentalising my experience.

Once I read about structural dissociation and the division of the personality into Apparently Normal Personalities (ANPs) and Emotional Personalities (EPs), it began to make sense of the shifts in identity I had and the conflict between different parts. Once I began to understand a little neuroscience and grasped the fundamental concept of neuroplasticity, I started to have hope for recovery. Once I realised that there are thousands of people who are opposed to the 'medical model' because it breeds hopelessness and despair and a dependence on life-shortening drugs, I began to have hope for recovery through resolving trauma, not just medicating it. Once I began to understand that I am not alone, that my experiences have a name and that there is a wealth of both clinical literature and research about the way I and others like me cope with life, I began to feel I belonged. Educating myself about trauma, abuse, dissociation, attachment, neuroscience and therapy has given me knowledge, and knowledge is power.

3. Choose your own label

Labels are descriptions, shortcuts to understanding. They can be both helpful and unhelpful. I wish I'd come across the label 'dissociative identity disorder' sooner. It would have explained so much. Instead, I was alone with my experiences, sliding in and out of various expressions of myself and lacking a coherent sense of self or memory of my actions. It was terrifying not to know what was going on. I thought I was simply 'mad.'

Madness is another label, usually a pejorative one, and in contrast to it 'dissociative identity disorder' was a huge improvement. It told me that I wasn't crazy and that I had a series of experiences and symptoms which other people had too and that trauma was at the root of it. But then the pull is towards the label. I would read about DID and frown at the disparities between other people's experiences and mine. Maybe I'm not 'proper DID.' I wondered what it would be like to meet other people with DID. When I did, they were reassuringly normal—people with careers, in relationships, with children, with the same sets of neuroses and anxieties as everyone else, but with this usually hidden, subset of experiences and the agony of trauma behind their eyes. Then there were others with DID where multiplicity was the central core of their daily existence, who spoke about 'alters,' 'systems,' and 'fronting.'

I wanted to hold my label lightly, as an explanation of my worldview but not as an identity. I started to think that we each need to choose our own label, the label that will best help us navigate the life we choose to lead and, in my case, the label that will best expedite my recovery. I can adapt my label to my audience: 'complex PTSD' is more acceptable in some medical circles; 'traumatised' covers a multitude of eventualities; a seemingly scientific but meaningless 'neurological disorder' is effective when I want to be vague. I don't have to justify myself to anyone; I can choose a label if it protects and assists me but equally I can disregard labels altogether if they harm me or inhibit me. DID is just a label—it's not who I am.

4. Embrace truth rather than avoidance and denial

I didn't grow up in an environment of truth. When people abuse children, truth is not their friend. Truth would speak of evil acts. So abusers deal in untruths, half-truths, distortions. Truth therefore is a slippery ideal for many of us who had to collude with the untruths of our abusers just to survive. Even when some of us spoke out and told the truth, few of us were believed. For many of us, we doubt what truth is because it has been distorted by adults in our life who insisted that we were lying or fantasising or making things up. Truth is a hard concept for us to grasp. But the atmosphere we breathed in as children shaped our brains. Dissociation is the flip side to avoidance and denial. It says, 'That didn't happen' or 'That didn't happen to me.' Avoidance tempts us away from painful realities by overworking, or addiction, or the fantasy-land of over-elaborated personalities.

Embracing truth as our friend can feel an impossible task. But I have found it essential on the pathway towards recovery. I have had to overcome the denial that says that nothing bad happened. I have had to challenge the lie that my abusers are good and I am the bad one. I have had to confront my tendency to keep on avoiding the trauma, all reminders, all my parts, all my emotions, just to function.

The pathway to recovery is one which embraces truth, even the truth about my abusers, even the truth that I am not shameful and disgusting, even the truth that bad things did happen. But unlike deception, and denial, and avoidance, truth does offer a way out: through acceptance, through compassion, through empathy, there is a new way to live based on 'this is true' where the hard emotions of grief can be felt, and having been felt, begin to melt away. Truth offers me stark realities about my family of origin but it has taken greater courage to accept the truth that it is not who I am.

5. Bless that body

Self-harm, obesity, lack of exercise, lack of sleep, smoking, alcohol, drugs, tension, infections, disease and pain: these are just a few ways that our bodies continue to suffer. Back then, as a child, we had no choice in it. The abuse that was visited upon us through the medium of our physical bodies was beyond our power to control. We grew up learning that our bodies don't matter and that pain or discomfort are their normative modes of experience. We learn that our bodies are there to gratify others' needs and that they are worthless and undeserving in and of themselves.

So it's little wonder then that as adults we continue to treat our bodies the same way. Even noticing them, even drawing the focus of our minds onto ourselves, can be overwhelming to the point of switching. We coped 'back then' by distancing ourselves from our bodies and they have repaid us with somatic flashbacks and long-term chronic disease. But the abuse isn't over until the fat lady sings. Or rather, the abuse isn't over until we start to notice our bodies, care for our bodies, resource our bodies, rest our bodies, even love them.

Eight years ago I didn't see the link between my trauma, the dissociation, and my body. Trauma, I reasoned, is a mental thing. So what has trauma got to do with the body? I continued my avoidance of it for as long as I could. But eventually, several years later than the ideal, I began to appreciate that trauma is visited upon the body, and trauma returns via the body. My heart rate, my cortisol levels, my insomnia, my pain—all the symptoms of unprocessed trauma—are experienced in my body. I needed a fundamental shift in my attitude to this clump of cells and tissues that somehow, despite my greatest efforts, was keeping me alive. I had to become outraged at the way that my body had been treated and I had to make an active, daily choice not to abuse it any longer. I just wish I'd started longer ago.

6.   Learn to manage triggers

Triggers are like little psychic explosions, reminders of the trauma that catapult us back to the 'there-and-then.' In the blink of an eye, a trigger evokes a body memory, a flashback, a switch to a traumatised part of our self. Triggers seem beyond our control. The traumatic experience of powerlessness then also fuels our experience of triggers so that after the first flashback, the first body memory, we are convinced that we are helpless to cope with them. But that's our first mistake. Triggers can be managed and we can learn how—just as we can learn to play a musical instrument or speak a foreign language. Through practice, through dogged, determined application of our minds to the task, we can learn to manage them.

I wish I'd known that eight years ago. I wish it hadn't taken me so long to begin to understand how our front thinking brain shuts down and our back survival brain takes over. I wish I hadn't been fooled, by the memory of powerlessness, into believing that I am actually powerless now to act. Learning to manage triggers—at least most of the time—has given me back my life, enabled me to return to work, and helped me to engage collaboratively with the multitude of parts that make up my personality. If you can learn to manage triggers, you can concentrate on the other aspects of recovery. But until you do, life will be a chaotic struggle for safety and stability that leaves you back at square one however much other progress you try to make.

7.   Exchange powerlessness for responsibility

I would argue that the core essence of trauma—that series of events that led to us developing a dissociative disorder in the first place—is powerlessness. And recovery from trauma therefore is as much about overcoming that powerlessness as it is about resolving traumatic memories or integrating the multiple parts of the personality. Powerlessness tells us, first of all, that recovery isn't possible. It whispers to us daily that this is for life, that it won't get better than this, that we'd better make the most of being DID and just learn to live with it because we can't be any different.

Powerlessness manifested for me in a number of ways: in struggling to erect and maintain boundaries in my relationships, especially with people who had abused me; in believing that I could do nothing at all to reduce my physical symptoms of pain and insomnia and terrorised hypervigilance; in the dynamics of my relationships, of obsequiousness towards authority figures or competitiveness with peers. Powerlessness told me that I would never recover, or work, or have fulfilling relationships again. But powerlessness lies.

Powerlessness is a temporary experience that belonged back there-and-then. Once I realised that it is a state of mind rather than a true reflection of reality, I began to challenge the myths I had swallowed and I began to recover. But to do that I had to take responsibility: for myself, for my life, for my emotions, for my behaviour, for the different parts of my personality, for my reactions, for my triggers, for my recovery. I had to decide that, although other people had caused my DID to develop, only I could recover from it. I could enlist the help and support of my husband, and of two therapists, but they couldn't do it for me. They couldn't rescue me from my feelings and they couldn't tell me what to do. I had to take responsibility for the rest of my life and so my recovery would succeed or fail based on my willingness to determine my life, rather than allowing it to be determined by other people, especially people from the past.

At times it felt as if I would be crushed by the enormity of the responsibility for managing my own recovery but that too was a lie: all I had to do, every single day, was point myself in the right direction and take one or two steps forwards, accepting that I was definitely powerless then but I'm no longer powerless now.

8.   Stop the self-blame

When your core belief is that you are worthless and shameful and toxic and bad, 'self-blame' appears in the guise of 'truth.' If I really am bad, then what could be wrong with attacking myself for being it? Surely, if I didn't, I risked being even worse? Who knows what would happen, what atrocities I would commit, what relationships I would contaminate with my inherent badness, if I didn't keep it in check with vicious, self-directed attacks? By censuring myself, surely I was being good? And the abuse—well, surely that was my fault, because I am bad, and I deserved it? And if I doubt myself, if I pick apart and undermine every action and conversation, then surely that will rein in my latent, shameful hubris which would otherwise result in delusions of grandeur that I can get things right?

Self-blame masquerading as truth, self-abuse masquerading as discipline, self-doubt masquerading as the brakes: this was the norm for me. But I wish I'd dealt with it sooner. If I got ten out of ten for a spelling test at school, I was told that I was big-headed. It was ok to succeed but wrong to admit to it. It was ok to work hard but wrong to enjoy the fruits of it. This pervasive negativity strangled my self-confidence. I ended up at Cambridge University with a profound conviction that I must be there due to an administrative error.

But I didn't realise what damage I was doing by parroting the negativity of my upbringing. I didn't realise that I was locking myself in a cage, thinking I was doing it for my own good, to prevent me causing harm to others. I had to make a conscious choice to drop the self-blame, to shift it onto the people who deserved it and to give myself a break. I had to choose daily not to destroy myself with critical self-talk or limit myself with misguided doubt. The result has not been what I feared—an abuser towards others. The result has been that I have stopped being an abuser towards myself. The road to recovery involves allowing ourselves to be successful and breaking through the limiting chains of our invalidating upbringing. It is ok to succeed.

9.   Learn to think and feel, and preferably at the same time

I always considered myself to be doing ok on the thinking front. I thought: in the shower, on the loo, in bed, in the car. I thought, and thought, and thought some more. And I really did believe that I could think my way out of my problems—if only I could think clearly enough. Cognitive Behavioural Therapy just gave me more thoughts to think.

In other words, my front left brain was heavily developed, but I lacked self-reflective thinking. I couldn't think outside the confines of my own head. I couldn't mentalise and step back from the thought processes I was caught up in. Thinking was only going to get me so far and mentalising, or metacognition—thinking about thinking—was needed for me to progress. I had to break through the closed-loop system of the thoughts I was thinking and be able to reflect on it and wonder why I was thinking those thoughts and not some others. I had to stop being victim to my endless runaway thoughts, believing them as if they were always true.

I also had to learn how to feel. My daily emotional repertoire after my breakdown involved distress, panic, anxiety and terror. But I diligently avoided actually feeling those emotions: I self-harmed, I drank, I took tablets, I distracted myself in whatever way I could. I did anything other than feel the feelings and sit with those feelings. And I certainly didn't think about or reflect on my emotional experiences. I used my thinking to avoid my feeling. And when feelings burst all over me in a moment of unguardedness, I did my best afterwards not to think about what had happened, what had led up to that explosion, what had triggered that catastrophe.

I only began to see real progress when I understood for the first time that both thoughts and feelings are just experiences in my mind, that they are not 'true' in and of themselves and that they won't hang around forever. I began to make progress when I learned to be mindful and to notice my thoughts and feelings, to stand back from them and be curious and not to kickstart a second wave of thinking and feeling based on chastising myself for having 'wrong' thoughts or 'wrong feelings.'

Mindfulness, or to use Daniel Siegel's term 'mindsight,' is a powerful tool towards recovery and even integration. Being able to slow down my thoughts and just notice them; being able to be curious about why I'm feeling distressed, rather than just being swallowed up by shame for attention-seeking or self-pity; being able to just notice that my feeling of anxiety is like ants crawling in my tummy and that it's in motion so it too will soon pass... These have become powerful tools for managing the riot of thoughts and feelings that were originally split apart from each other. When I can both think in a reflective way and feel in a curious way and I can do both at the same time, I know that I'm making progress.

10. Pursue recovery as my best revenge

As a victim of organised abuse in childhood, I have been wronged in many ways. I've often found that discourses on 'forgiveness' are for many survivors frustrating at best and insulting at worst. I'm interested in recovery and I'm interested in how I can turn the rage that is latent within me towards that recovery. I want recovery to be my best revenge.

So many times the rightful anger that we have because of what happened to us is turned either against ourselves in vicious self-hatred or against 'safe' targets in the here-and-now: it is easier to vent against our therapist, the NHS, the police, the justice system, or society at large than it is to feel those feelings towards the people from childhood who should have loved us rather than abused us. There are many things that therapists, the NHS, the police and the government should do better. But I have benefited most from not getting caught up in a battle for services and engaging my energy instead in the hard work of therapy. I have decided that the best revenge I can have is to recover as completely as I can and to help others do the same. It won't undo the wrongs of the past but I refuse to let my abusers succeed in trashing the rest of my future.

The abuse I suffered wasn't anyone's fault but the people who abused me. So often in the media, like in Rochdale, we see statutory agencies bearing the brunt of public blame for the organised abuse of children, as if they were the ones committing the acts. I don't doubt that there were—and there probably always will be—serious failings and missed opportunities for children to be protected. It's a good thing when Serious Case Reviews provide concrete suggestions for how children can be better protected in the future. But the Head of

Children's Services in Haringey is not the person who abused Baby P. If we focus our anger towards the wrong people, we will end up in a futile battle to get people from today to take responsibility for what other people of yesterday did. I just want to recover: that's where I'm going to focus my energies and my recovery will be, for me at least, my best revenge.

Volume Two

CHAPTER ELEVEN

Developing compassion for parts

'She is the hated child, sitting across from me, mocking me.'

I didn't write this, but when I read it, in an email sent to me by a fellow survivor, the words resonated with my own self-experience. And many of us know it: the dirty, persistent self-hatred that we have for ourselves, these 'parts' of ourselves that we have so needed to disown that many of them have become completely 'other', separate, 'not me'.

In dissociative identity disorder, our divided psyche exists because our experiences were so traumatic and overwhelming that we couldn't 'integrate' them. Instead, we hold these discrete self-states as separate strands of our consciousness. Over time, many of them took on autonomous, distinct characteristics and developed into 'alter personalities'. It is a way of distancing ourselves from the trauma; it is also a way of distancing ourselves from our feelings, our vulnerabilities and our needs.

At first, my awareness of these 'other' parts of me was via other people, who recounted to me what they had said, what they had done, in those time blanks where I was unaware. Even then, I pushed it away. I didn't really want to know. It sounded mad—it was mad!— and I didn't want to hear that a 'young' part of me calling herself

'Diddy' had been distressed and distraught. I didn't want to hear that a belligerent, 'adolescent' part called 'Switch' had been wanting to self-harm. I didn't want to know that an unnamed part had sat for hours twiddling the thread of a blanket, impervious to touch or words or eye-contact. I was less disturbed when I found that in my time blanks I had been writing, or cleaning. But even then I didn't really want to know what happened when I wasn't 'here', when I wasn't 'myself'. Perhaps if I didn't know, it would just go away.

After my breakdown in 2005, the not-knowing became more difficult as the time-blanks increased and the invisible activities made themselves visible in the aftermath of overdoses or fugues. Lost in the countryside, I still had to navigate myself back again. The emotions still had to settle and they lingered like reflux in my soul. The not-knowing about who I was and what I did when 'not-me' was convenient at first in evading the embarrassment of my actions but it soon became inconvenient. It caused stress to people who cared about me and did nothing to help restabilise my life.

So I had to start to figure out who these other 'parts' of me were, and I didn't want to. Firstly, there was the denial—'They're not real, I'm making it up, you're making it up'. Then the avoidance—'Just ignore them and they'll go away.' And then the sickening reality that there really were times when I didn't know what I was doing and yet there was this trail of evidence that I'd been doing something and it wasn't at all the kind of thing I usually did... I eventually hit up against the obviousness of 'me-not-me' and realised that I had to take it seriously, had to face it and confront it and deal with it, rather than pretending like a toddler that peekaboo makes you invisible.

But I hated them. I really, truly hated them. I did not want to be vulnerable as 'Diddy' any more than I wanted to be twisted-up as 'Switch'. I just wanted to be me—capable, competent and professional me. Except, starting in 2005, I seemed to have lost that capable, competent me and my days were a mashed-up existence of here-and-not-here, in-and-out, me-and-not-me. I thought for a while that if I denied these 'others' strongly enough, then they really would go away and leave me alone, and back would come Competent, Capable Carolyn and all would be well with the world. Except it didn't quite happen like that. I'd had a breakdown for a reason, and there was no going back.

So I had to get to know them. Even 'the hated child, sitting across from me, mocking me.' To be honest, all of them were hated; it felt as if most of them were mocking me. There was the high-speed chatter of acerbic criticism; the intolerant disgust of silent pouting; the delirious scream of all-out rage; the silence of stuck-still terror. These were the voices of the 'others'—to a degree embodied in my imagination, but ever-present, like white noise, oppressive and unalone. I wanted it to stop. All day long: screaming. All day long: a wail of unmitigated suffering. All day long: the hot-breath snarl of the malicious critic, exposing yet another failure. I knew that they were not 'real people' with three-dimensional bodies. I also knew that they were not just 'voices' or a clattering of meaningless, disconnected thoughts. I knew, without knowing the right name for it, that these were parts of me. But I also knew that to talk about them as real would invite the noose-label of 'schizophrenia' and that its inevitable medication would give no space for thought or processing or reason. I had to hold my parts as 'feeling real' whilst accepting that they were not—that they were parts of me, not other people, and not psychotic intrusions either. And all the time, on the outside, look normal.

Therapy started the dialogue. It was curious at first to realise that this person sitting opposite me had just been conversing with me, but me-as-other-me. At first, I tried not to think about it. It felt too shameful. But over time, as I realised that she wasn't fazed by it, and that I wasn't being shamed for it, or punished, I began to allow the reality to sink in. It was undeniable. There I sat, with just void stretching behind me for the last twenty minutes, and she was telling me things that I-as-not-me had told her, that only I would know. She had clearly been talking to me, just not me-as-me. And it was startling to be told about these nuances of me-as-not-me: familiar characteristics, but stretched taut, like a rubber band. Switch was clearly a part of me but an extreme version: vulnerable, prescient, outraged, hurting. He could communicate what I was feeling deep in my guts, in a way that I hadn't even begun to recognise for myself, let alone share with another. He carried memories that I did not, with a sharp, high definition reality to them, especially the emotions. He knew other parts of me. He was able to lean forwards into relationship in a way that I could not. So my first real introduction to this Switch part of me was as he was reflected back to me from my therapist's experience, and then my husband's. It took a long time to be able to hear it, and accept that this was me, albeit me-as-not-me, that they were referring to.

Then came internal dialogue. It seemed utterly stupid to begin with. How are you supposed to 'communicate inside'? At first I held back not so much out of ignorance for 'technique', and fear that nothing would happen, but more out of fear that it would. I still didn't want to accept that I had 'parts'. What if they did indeed talk back to me? Would that prove I was mad? I read others' accounts and it seemed like some people could hold an open dialogue, saying things to themselves and clearly hearing a reply. It didn't work like that for me. I had to hunt for the sense inside. I had to learn to finely adjust my antenna and seek out the signal. The communication within was more in the rumble of shifting tectonic plates, more in the pain that streaked suddenly upwards, more in the wave of emotion that stung my eyes. Only gradually was I able to begin to put these sensations into words. It took a number of years before I could look inside, listen, and then say, 'I think Switch is feeling...' Communication is not easy. But it is essential.

Words have always been my thing, so I let words run riot to aid this internal dialogue. I would journal daily, sometimes several times daily, and let a rip-roaring splurge erupt from within me—writing anything, everything, asking questions, answering them, going with the flow, using imagery, writing out imaginary dialogue, seeking an impression from within. It didn't have to make sense. I was just showing myself that I was willing to search for myself, that I was willing to listen to myself, that I was willing to hear. Sometimes I would use more than words—diagrams and headlines of elusive thoughts drawn together on A3 sheets of paper with interconnecting lines drawn in different colours: anything to get my usually-dormant right brain into action. The purpose wasn't the end product: the purpose was the communication. Sometimes I would 'lose time' as another part took over; other times I would be vaguely aware that I wasn't quite 'myself', that I felt distant and derealised, and that I was observing myself write. Sometimes, when that happened, I didn't know what it was that I was writing, until I read it through again afterwards. It became a way of practising switching in and out of parts whilst remaining co-conscious—allowing myself to be the whole of me, and be conscious of being the whole of me, rather than squirrelling myself away into shameful obscurity.

And she sat across from me, the hated child, mocking me. Gradually I learned to just let her be, and not try to change her. Not try to blot her out, or punish her for existing, or shame her into submission, or silence her with threats. Maybe she could just be. I realised what an abuser I was—to myself. Everything that I hated about the people who had dealt atrocities to me, I was doing to myself. I would shout at myself, hiss at myself, punish myself, yell at myself, torture myself, demean myself, humiliate myself, shame myself, scold myself, hurt myself, hate myself. I would do everything to myself that had been done to me by others. And if I was honest, I wanted other people to treat me well. I wanted them to love me. I wanted them to be kind towards me and give me a break. But fundamentally, towards myself, I wanted to be an abuser.

Then these two words, whispered in therapy, proffered as an alternative viewpoint: *self-compassion.*

I heard them, and nothing registered. They made no sense. I had a tonne of compassion—for others. Very little for fools (admittedly) but a lot for people who were hurting. And yet, strangely, I had none for myself. It hadn't even occurred to me that I could have it for myself. Compassion was what you had for other people—why would you have it for yourself? It felt selfish, and greedy, and indulgent, and glib. Self-compassion? Wouldn't that make me more bad? If I loosened the leash, if I gave myself a break, if I showed kindness and concern and empathy and love, wouldn't I be allowing the devil within me to take over and go berserk? I needed to be harsh towards myself: it was the only thing that held back my evil. I needed to criticise myself: who knows what mistakes I would make if I didn't punish myself cruelly for each tiny one. I needed to shout at myself: if I didn't, laziness would consume me and I would lay forever in an unwashed sprawl of slobbery on the sofa. When did compassion ever play a part? I survived what I survived because I had parents who loved me by beating me when I was bad, by punishing me when I was slack. They girdled my ego with criticism to keep it in check. That is how you're supposed to motivate, and restrain, and control, and direct. It worked for me...

Except, of course, it didn't. I grew up with DID. I grew up wanting to kill myself. I grew up with a self-loathing so massive that daily I plotted my own self-destruction. But old habits die hard. When you've been abused as a form of 'discipline', to make you 'good', it's hard to break away from the brainwashing that tells you that it was for your own good, and that if they didn't hurt you then you would be even 'badder' than you already are.

Believing that I was fundamentally bad, I accepted my parents' harsh discipline of me as love, which is what they said it was. I accepted that if they hadn't censured me for dropping 1.25% on a French exam, the next time I would have failed completely. When I won a place at Cambridge University, my mother comforted me: 'You didn't get in because you're clever. You only got in because you worked hard.' Had she not punished me for the failed marks in French, I wouldn't have been so industrious, and then I wouldn't have been able to trick the system to gain a place at a University where I wasn't clever enough to be. I had a lot to be grateful to her for.

And I accepted her techniques. Every failure, every missed punctuation mark on an essay, every question that I didn't immediately know the answer to, I berated myself for being lazy and stupid. And it worked. I did well. Until it didn't work, and I had a breakdown. Until I could bear being abused no longer.

It was several years into therapy though before the irony struck me: the irony that here I was, week after week, session after session, trying to put myself back together again, trying to heal from the abuse. I was trying to rebuild myself and integrate myself and establish a secure base within myself to go out and conquer the world, rather than accept defeat and commit suicide. I was trying to heal from abuse, and all the time I was still abusing myself. Still snarling at my struggles, still flipping out at a drink spill, still growling at my imperfections. Abuse, abuse, abuse. Back at me came this therapist, who wouldn't abuse me, wouldn't run me down, wouldn't growl at me or shout at me or shriek at me like a banshee, wouldn't accept that it was all my fault, wouldn't accept that I should have done something, wouldn't accept that I deserved it. I kept fighting her but eventually she began to win. They get you in the end, these therapists. They keep at you with their insistent, patient, pesky tenacity. They keep treating you with 'unconditional positive regard' and eventually you just have to throw your hands up and accept that you're never going to change their minds, because they're just too damn stubborn. An irresistible force meets an immovable object and *ker-bang!* suddenly it's *your* worldview that is changed.

What would it mean for me not to abuse myself? What would it mean for me to treat myself as I'm pleading for other people to treat me? What would it mean for me to draw a line in the sand, step over it, and say that I'm not going back? That the abuse is over, that I won't let anyone else abuse me now, not even me? What would that look like? What would it mean?

At first, it just meant terror. It was all unthinkable. It was a trick. It must be. Abuse was the one constant in my life, a reassuring backdrop. Awful—yes. Unbearable—of course. And yet always there. I couldn't imagine life without it. What would my voices say all day long? What would some of them do? I couldn't imagine it. I didn't want it. Better the devil I knew…

Powerlessness told me that I couldn't change it, that I couldn't live in a new world, a free world, a world without abuse. I can't. I didn't know why; I just knew it was true—I can't. Then that collision again, where I had to admit that my feelings are just feelings, and are meant to be felt. And truth is truth and is meant to be believed. And sometimes, just sometimes—'never the twain shall meet'. So on the one side, I felt that I couldn't imagine life without abuse. I felt that I could never manage to show myself compassion, and draw near to these other parts of me. And then the skull-cracking realisation that I wasn't powerless—I was powerful. I was powerful enough to keep ruining my life by perpetuating the abuse. And I was powerful enough to develop new habits, too, and end it.

'It is what it is' became a bit of a mantra. But I couldn't just say it—too many years of Sensorimotor Psychotherapy taught me this—no, I had to say it with a shrug of the shoulders. Not any shrug of the shoulders either. *That* shrug of the shoulders. That particular shrug of the shoulders that I learned as a way of resourcing myself, the feeling that I 'installed' in my memory of being competent and capable and able to choose, that I was my own master and commander, that I was in charge of my life, and if I didn't want to go there, didn't want to do that, didn't want to take that abuse any more...I just needed to do an upside-down smile and that shrug of the shoulders and say, 'It is what it is' and walk away. I could fail at something, mess something up, get something inside-out kind of wrong, and at the end of it I just needed to sigh, smile upside-down, shrug and say, 'Oh well, it is what it is.' End of. No more beating myself up. Just a shrug of my shoulders and a keen, heartfelt attitude towards myself of self-compassion and 'It's ok.'

Slowly, my attitude towards some of these other parts of me began to change. Perhaps there was nothing wrong with Diddy for being little, and vulnerable, and for needing. Perhaps it's normal to need. Perhaps I don't have to get cross with her like my mother got cross with me, to keep her neediness in check. Perhaps if I just sit down next her to her, sidle up to her, put an arm around her... perhaps then she might stop crying and she might be able to catch her breath and to be. The part of me that stiffens in shameful horror at spilling a drink: perhaps instead of the tirade inside that I feel at the stupidity, the clumsiness, the idiocy, the carelessness... perhaps instead I could just smile, and shrug my shoulders, say, 'It is what it is...' and help to clean up. And perhaps then the other parts, the ones who flail me furiously that I'm not good enough, and I don't do enough, and I don't know enough, and I'm not working hard enough... perhaps they'll learn from me and loosen up too. Perhaps we could all aim to work together a bit more. Isn't that what healing, and recovery, and integration is all about?

She sits across from me still, but she doesn't mock me as much. Slowly she's learning that I understand and that I care and that I won't hurt her. I won't hate her any more. At times I still get frustrated with her, and I don't get it right. But then it's her turn to roll her eyes, shrug her shoulders, and say, right back at me, with less than a growl but not quite yet a smile, 'It is what it is.'

CHAPTER TWELVE

Write to Life

Corned beef sandwiches

It was my first week at my third school. I was five, and I was in trouble. The previous day I had written beautifully, this teacher said, towering above me, massive and portentous. Now today I wasn't trying. *I was trying*, I wanted to say, but today the words wouldn't come. They were dry and scratchy and the paper looked so big, and I gnawed on myself with a fretful anxiety. I shouldn't be doing this, I'm going to be in trouble. When parents' evening came, there was my mother, stiletto heels, lipstick, imperious and withering. There was my father, jovial and terrifying, the One in Charge. My workbook, oversized, pages like the innards of toilet roll. The big loopy writing of a five-year-old, but a page of it, because I had been reading since I was two, and here was my tale of 'what we did at the weekend'. At home, afterwards, the gulping shock of reprimand, fear swooshing in my guts, a terrible, kill-me-now shame. At the weekend we'd had corned beef sandwiches for lunch, so that's what I'd written. But now: *Do not tell. Do not say that. Do not tell them anything, ever again. This is private, this is secret, this is family. Do not tell.*

The library

Jutting and beautiful, red bricks, hard edges. Inside, the smell of pages, the tall gloom of bookshelves, wonder upon wonder of books and secrets and smells and rustling. Pages turning. Discreet coughing. Books and books and the ceiling high above the clouds in this most wonderful of places. First some shopping, then the library. The biggest, bestest, wonderfullest library. Books everywhere. I wandered not in the children's section but up and down and in and out and round and through and everywhere, vast columns of books like giants' legs reaching up to the moon, and I wanted to live here forever, even when the crinkly woman told me to be quiet. I was being quiet, but she didn't believe me, because I was a child let loose. I couldn't stay in the children's corner with all these books out *here*. I wanted to eat them. Five years later, in another library, I was alone, forgotten by my mother, who had left without me. I didn't know what to feel. I wanted to stay forever and I wanted not to be forgotten and the collision inside me made me sick with fretfulness. *Please leave me here forever, but come back soon.*

Surreptitiously

I read sixty books in the first month of secondary school. We kept a log in a notebook, which ran out before half-term. Each week, a book review. *Surreptitiously*. There they were, the rebels, surrounded and overpowered, hands on heads, surrendered, lost. Stormtroopers everywhere. Somewhere, up in their sky, Luke discarded his light-sabre. All was lost. Hopeless. Defeat. Terror. The end of. But then, but then—*surreptitiously*. I didn't know what it meant. I savoured it, turned it over on my tongue. *Surreptitiously*. What kind of a word was this? What did it mean? How had I spent 11 years not knowing about it? *Surreptitiously*. Can you feel it, can you taste it, can you see how beautiful it is? Not just because it is, not just because it sizzles and pops and promises and slithers, but because at this moment, at this climax, at this point of utter, irrevocable doom, *surreptitiously* she removed her blaster. All these men fighting, all these stormtroopers fighting, the shrivelled, cackling Emperor, the gleaming, glistening Vader, oil-black and evil, and it's the damsel in distress who has the blaster and who *surreptitiously* removes it from its holster. *Surreptitiously*. She doesn't want to be caught. She doesn't want to be seen. But she doesn't freeze, she doesn't panic, she doesn't run, she doesn't cry. Just *surreptitiously*. What a word. What a moment. I want to write like that. I want to be the one who *surreptitiously* comes to the rescue. If only I could think like that, write like that, act like that, imagine like that. *Surreptitiously*. When they're hurting me, can I *surreptitiously* remove a blaster from its holster? What might happen if I did?

Mrs Lavender

I sat next to a boy called Simon Valentine. Later I would play golf with him, which he was good at, but for now he was the school *squit* whose punishment in English was to sit next to the school *swot*. He flicked his pen at me, rocked the table, and I tried to ignore him. There were words to read, and words to write. Our exam papers were back. And Mrs Lavender, this teacher who had let me run the school bookshop in her mobile classroom at lunchtime, this teacher with the aromatic purple name, who was neither fun nor furious… this teacher crouched down by the side of my desk. I worried that she would get pins and needles. She crouched for a very long time. She talked to me quietly. She leaned in closer than she had ever leaned in before. She said that I had a gift for writing. She said other things. And all while she must have had pins and needles in her legs. She said things that didn't make sense, because they were good. Something that stirred on the inside of her moved across the tiny tiny space between us (less space than I'd ever had without being hurt), and stirred me too. Something about my writing. Something about possibilities. Something about hope. Something good. But still I worried about her pins and needles.

Brunner's books

I loved that bookshop. Mr Brunner, with the half-moon specs, the balding pate, the unassuming kindliness. He was my hero. Every week, he said hello and even seemed pleased to see me. He ordered me books, weeks before they were published. I went in on the day that he said they *might* arrive: couldn't guarantee it, couldn't make promises, not now like Amazon Prime. This was the old days, back when we had squitty little bookshops down squitty little roads in squitty little market towns. I didn't mind if the books hadn't come when he said they *might*. It meant I could go back the next time. The bookshop was so squishy-squashy, books wedged into cubbyholes of shelves, spines out, no front covers. This was a bookshop for serious browsers. For me. My section of favourites, most of which I owned already, took up an armful of shelf space. But I looked at each one, over and over again, even the ones I had at home. Sometimes he asked about school. Mostly he was just there. Safe. I could look at the books, smell them, touch them, study them, listen to them. They sound different when you zizz the pages with your thumb: the newest books are stiff at the spine; the cheapest books drone like bees. Just that sound was enough to make my heart sing, with Mr Brunner quietly behind his till, tidying, sorting, pinging the register, polite chat to his customers, not minding me there in the background, ekeing out each moment. He showed me catalogues when we couldn't find the book I wanted. Publishers' catalogues, huge long lists with publication dates and codes. They were beautiful. One day I wanted my book to be in those lists. One day I wanted Mr Brunner to sell it. One day I wanted to be Mr Brunner. Because in the world of books, none of the bad stuff happened and I could be the other person that I was not, without anyone knowing. How would I have survived if there hadn't been books, and libraries, and bookshops?

Dear John

I wrote bad poems and submitted them for publication. I pored over the *Writers' and Artists' Yearbook* to find where to send them. I handwrote the letter, and bought stamps with my pocket money. My parents laughed. Three weeks later, the first envelope came. It was sitting on the kitchen table, my first piece of post. Mockery fluttered in the air like a bird in the chimney, shitting everywhere. I opened it. Mirth, and contempt. It said no. 'Dear John' my parents said, and erupted in glee. 'Dear John' they said, shaking their heads and laughing as they left the room. I felt my own stupidity. I awaited the other two letters with dread. Was it worth this humiliation? 'Dear John' hung in the air like the stench of cabbages, the taunt whenever the post arrived. 'Told you so—dear John' when the others did. How stupid of me even to try.

The Elite

I wrote my first book in lunchtimes at school. In a little room off the library, I tried to hide from my peers. I didn't understand what friendship was. I didn't know how to be liked. I couldn't bear the cruelty. I just wanted to write. I dreamt of appearing on 'Wogan' as the youngest ever novelist. It was finished when I was 12, a sci-fi escapade, the good guys fleeing the 'N-Forcers', the bad guys inflicting needless cruelty simply because they could. It needed a second draft. I kept on writing to keep on avoiding: the library was the only place away from the cattiness of pubescent girls. I didn't know how to be. There I was, in the library, writing my story, but even that became my torment: classmates came and stood at the door and mocked me. This is just the way it is, I thought. I will always be mocked. And I will shrug my shoulders and keep doing it, because that's just the way it is too. The Elite were the good guys, my underdog freedom fighters, chasing through the galaxy, trying to escape for no other reason than because they were being chased. Which felt like me.

Shortlisted

We'd been there once before, to see a man called Archie compete in a weightlifting tournament. It was stupefyingly dull. A bald man clapped chalk on his hands, flexed his muscles, tried to lift a bar of weights, succeeded or failed, and walked away. Followed by another bald man. That was all. What a waste of a Cambridge College. But this time the curtain backdrop was gold and a lectern stood pompous in centre stage. I'd had a letter—I had been shortlisted for a short story competition—and here we were at Robinson College for the winners to be announced. When the envelope arrived, and I read aloud its contents in the kitchen at home, trying oh so hard to sound uneager, there were noises of acknowledgement, mutterings about what day it was, parking in Cambridge, and then: 'You won't have won. You're only there to make up the numbers.' Was it worth the hassle, the parking, the night out, the effort, just to make up the numbers? I wanted to go anyway, even if just to be a number, because it was a Cambridge college, it was a writer's competition, it was different, it was a world that I dreamt about. Surely we could find a way to park, if only to make up the numbers? I felt ashamed that I still hoped I would win, but I didn't dare admit it—hubris, pride, arrogance, stupidity. *Dear John*—remember? My mother took me—it was only to make up the numbers, and I wasn't going to win—remember? And she was right. She was always right. I didn't win, but I saw what a winner looked like and they didn't look that different to me. Did they already know, or was it a shock to them? Why did they have both parents, two siblings and a grandmother all in tow? Had they all thought that they too were there just to make up the numbers?

Sunday tea

Sunday afternoons, log fire, curtains closed heavy against the rain, and I've been in my room for a long time, perfecting it. Getting ready for school tomorrow, parents doing the crossword, and I sit at the dining room table now, the don't-scratch-it-mahogany, the chairs that fart when you sit on them, and I write it all out onto thin-lined paper with the splodgy blue fountain pen because we can't submit homework in biro. When I've finished, I want to show it to someone because although it is partially plagiarised, the execution is still original. She's stuck with her crossword, so my mother agrees to read it. A wait like suspended breath until she's finished it. She goes back to her crossword, passes it to me sideways, and exhales disapproval. 'You're not right in the head,' she says, and I know she's got a point but I still didn't want to hear it. I abandon it, the short story of two spinsters hosting afternoon tea, the aroma of almonds, the young guest naïve and why wouldn't he be? Who knows that cynanide smells of almonds? Who would think that these old women, prim and lacy and Miss-Marple-meets-Bakewell-Tart, would intend to eat him? Only my deranged mind, but I needed to write it. As my mother discards it, my shame sticks in my throat like dry toast. There is something wrong with my head, and here is the proof. This story doesn't belong here, with the fire and crossword, with fondant fancies and Ski Sunday. What is wrong with me that I write stuff like this?

A grief ago

I sat on a narrowboat with *How Poetry Works*. It was electrifying. I hated poetry—didn't understand it. But this book talked about paradigms. It talked about Dylan Thomas—some Welsh poet, whoever he was (I hated poetry—didn't understand it)—saying 'a grief ago' rather than 'a week ago' or 'a year ago'. Isn't that brilliant? It was like on a slot machine—apples, cherries, bananas, oranges, all spinning around on their own intrinsic paradigm. Days, weeks, years, griefs—what's it gonna be? You could pick anything and bring it alive. You could change the rules. You didn't have to be right. You could do to language whatever you wanted to. You wouldn't get into trouble. You wouldn't be wrong. You wouldn't be the utter shite, waste of space, Dear John loser that you'd always been, just making up the numbers, being flattered by Mrs Lavender (probably as a way of getting back at your mother, whom she hated), crazily thinking you could write a book at 12. A grief ago. All the grief inside me, this marmitey, repulsive broth of feeling—all this grief that I didn't know was grief—spat out and sizzled at me on this longboat on the River Avon. Possibilities. Maybe I could go to a Cambridge college to be a student, and not just to make the numbers up or watch bald men clap chalk. If you can write 'a grief ago', then anything is possible, isn't it?

Penultimate pallor

I sit outside the room, at the top of a staircase, off a quintessential Cambridge college courtyard, staring blankly, a white piece of paper with inkshapes on it called 'words'. They make no sense. Like the 5-year-old with the starchy scrapbook paper where words wouldn't come, these words won't form thoughts in my mind. It is a poem. I have twenty minutes to read it and think about it before the next stage of my interview. I hate poetry still, despite a narrowboat ago. The early part of the interview is conversational, directed towards two essays that I've already submitted. 'So what?' one of the interviewers says, and I've never really thought that before. Surely auxiliaries are interesting and important because they are auxiliaries—in sixth form the cheer was for the use of the word 'auxiliary', and no one ever said 'So what?' My brain stretches taut with the thinking. Words. So what?

What next? And then what? And why? And how does that work? And why does it matter? Words about words—a searching, penetrating, naked-making interview. And then a question about the penultimate line and the word 'pallor'. In my stress, in my stretched-out mind still reeling from 'So what?', I struggle to think. Which is the penultimate line? The last one, or the one before the last one? Of what, of this?— this 'poem'? Pallor? Why are they talking about 'pallor'? Gently they prompt me—think of the Latin, think of its etymology. I think, and think some more, and my ignorance doesn't seem to disgust them as it would my mother, but they let me run with their thoughts and encourage the excitement in my bowels, the erupting pleasure that here are people who would be equally entranced by 'a pallor ago' if that's what I want to write. That pleasure seems to dance in the dusty light between us and they're not annoyed or displeased or mocking or contemptuous, but somehow, despite my ignorance, they seem to think that I can learn and that I can think and that there is potential. Pallor and pallid and white—and all I had seen was the white space around squiggles that were words, but here was a chance to dance with words and I wasn't mocked for my stupidity, and I leaped inside at this world of words where people jiggled with the same jiggledy delight as I did and I wanted it, like I'd never wanted anything else before. 'You won't get in,' said my mother.

Industry not intelligence
It was a blue Vauxhall Astra with a beautifully symmetrical number plate, and it had recovered from the dent in the side when I'd driven— intentionally—into a ditch on my second driving lesson. A car had come spinning around the corner, out of control, twirling like a coin in the drizzle on a glistening B-road, and instinctively, just in time, I had steered out of the way, between the zebra posts, and into long flowering grasses, right into a ditch. We ended up at 45 degrees and it had never occurred to me before how difficult it might be to open the driver's door when you're tilted in a ditch. Now, a year later, we were driving the same route again, towards Cambridge, through the villages parallel to the A14, and the roads were dry and I was weeks

from going to University. We were going to buy things I needed—a ridiculous, fustian, up-itself College gown and—more usefully—an ironing board. I was driving, as I always did; my mother was in the passenger seat. 'You didn't get into Cambridge because you're clever,' she said. 'You only got in because you worked hard.' I didn't argue— who could argue with her logic? I *had* worked hard, and *of course* I wasn't clever—silly old Dear John who went to awards ceremonies to make the numbers up. I was going to Cambridge, now, to make the numbers up again, and anyone who can't remember in an interview which is the penultimate line and doesn't know the etymology of 'pallor' is eminently stupid. And what did I want with an English degree anyway? I could read, but I couldn't write. People with English degrees end up as teachers—wouldn't that be a comfort, to be a teacher like my mother? My grandad, the one who raped me, wanted to be a journalist but ended up as a bricklayer because of the war. My mother was a PE teacher who had wanted to be a cricketer. Everyone hopes for something better than what they really are, and so I would never be a writer, just a reader.

I want to be a writer
After my first year at College, I couldn't bear to go home: thick-pile carpet, overbearing wallpaper, the suffocation of something that I couldn't quite know. I rented a room in a College hostel: high Edwardian ceilings, a square bay out onto College grounds, the echoey clanks from other inmates' doors and cold draughts even in Summer. Mike Gatting being bowled clean off a leg-break by Shane Warne: *that* Summer. I read Stephen Fry and *Fever Pitch*, guilty and unallowable in a Cambridge English literature curriculum. And I began to think: what do I really want? My mother stopped by one day, licked her tongue around at my untidiness, brought chicken-in-breadcrumbs from Marks and Spencers, which I turned into sandwiches. And foolishly I said to her, *I want to be a writer*. Just that, nothing else—a casual, throw-about comment, like *Gooch needs a good innings* but suddenly a switch, like Bilbo coveting the Ring and viciousness erupts. *We haven't paid for you to come here for you to waste your life writing*. And 'proper jobs' and 'earn a living' and 'be respectable' and 'don't let us down'

and this whirling, frenzied, dervish explosion of wrath at me. And the fear in it. The fear in me, but the fear in her too—fear that I would tell, perhaps, fear that I would say things that couldn't be said, that shouldn't be said, that—over her dead body—wouldn't be said? Who do I think I am? And there we go again, and it's this 'not right in the head' thing and suddenly, fabulously, I fight back *just a little*. I soon crumble because what is it, after all, to write, when you're not a writer, and you're only here by accident, and you're just making the numbers up, and you're not right in the head? How hard is it ever to break away from that voice, that sly, seductive, shaming voice, of the mother who knows best and *is* best and to whom you shall forever more show your allegiance and your gratitude by Never Writing, lest truth be told and all of it comes out about The Things That Happened? For a fleeting moment, I see it: the straitjacket she keeps me in, to make sure that I don't tell, but for twenty years it bounces back, hard as a cricket ball: the unassuaged guilt of the bad daughter, the unloving daughter, the uncaring, evil, betraying daughter, who would write about corned beef sandwiches. The words shimmer out of being on the page, because who am I to think that I can write? But then, quicker this time, comes that moment—just a glittering, etched-in-beauty moment—when I know that it is who I am and I'm allowed to and it's not my bad. And so: I will write.

CHAPTER THIRTEEN

Making the most of therapy

Y ou've come a long way. Misdiagnoses, mistreatment, maltreatment even—but eventually you're here. You've found a therapist willing to work with you—either privately or on the NHS—and so now you're expecting it just to happen. Right?

Wrong! Getting good therapy is an essential step in recovery from complex trauma and dissociative disorders but just turning up doesn't, in and of itself, make things 'better'. Therapy is not something that is 'done' to us, like radio therapy. It's not a case of sitting comfortably and letting the therapist do the work. In fact, in many ways, it's exactly the opposite. For therapy to be effective, we need to actively engage in it. But however much we know we might need it, however much we hope it will be effective, it's still the case that therapists have been to 'therapy school' to know what they're doing but we haven't been to 'client school' to know how to make best use of it.

And, let's face it—there's not much of it. It might be for just an hour or two a week, minus holidays, minus cancelled sessions due to illness or bereavement or accident. It may last just six weeks or six months or two years—however long it's for, invariably it's not long enough. So it's imperative we make the most of those precious hours we have, however few there are. Because, ultimately, research shows (Brand et al, 2012) that therapy is effective and for many of us it's not only our best chance but our only chance to get life back together again.

So what can we do to make the most of therapy?

1. Make it a priority

The first session or two can seem vitally important but it's easy to slip into an easy complacency once we're underway. We have a lot of reasons, unconsciously, to want to avoid it—we're vulnerable, we're talking about difficult subjects, it's bringing up painful feelings—and occasionally that means that we don't give it the priority in our week that it deserves. Right from the off, I put my sessions in my calendar weeks or even months in advance and everything else had to flow around it, even working full time. It was over seven years before I first voluntarily skipped a session—and that in itself was therapeutic because I was going on my first 'proper' holiday. But apart from that, my sessions take priority over everything else in my calendar. However ill I am feeling, however badly I slept, however busy I am at work—my sessions take priority. Everything else can wait: healing cannot.

2. Get in the zone

My sessions don't start at 10.30am on a Tuesday morning. My sessions 'start' in one sense on a Monday evening. These evenings too are usually sacrosanct—time to journal, to think, to plan how I'm going to use the session. And the next morning, I try wherever possible to allow myself space before the session starts, and after it has ended. When I had young children, that space was created by leaving early and going to sit in a coffee shop for an hour beforehand to 'get my head together'. I would read through my journals from the week before, my journals from during the week, I would sketch out things I needed to focus on. Whenever I skimped on this, whenever I didn't take the time to pull myself out of 'normal' life and allow myself some time in this emotional airlock, the sessions were never as productive. Sometimes, out of avoidance, I would find myself getting busy with stuff that I really didn't need to be busy with, and then, finding myself running late, I would speed to therapy and turn up in a hyperaroused state. It was never the best way to start, to already be out of my window of tolerance.

Punctuality is key. When my therapy was an hour's journey away and accessible only via The World's Busiest Road, I would leave two hours for the journey, just in case. Occasionally, an accident or hold-up meant that I did only arrive with minutes to spare—if I hadn't left so early, I would have missed my session entirely. Most of the time I had an hour to kill but I could use it productively sat somewhere with my journal, planning my session. Better early than never.

3.   Plan how to spend your session and take the driver's seat
It can be galling to realise that your therapist is not omniscient and even more galling if they operate on a 'led by the client' basis and are waiting for you to kick things off. Before I understood it, sometimes it struck me that perhaps my therapist was senile—could she not remember what we talked about last week? Sometimes I thought it was because she was disgusted—she could remember only too clearly what we had talked about last week. Sometimes it seemed that she was lazy—why couldn't she make more of an effort and think up something to say rather than always relying on me?! And sometimes I thought that she was just clueless and didn't know what to say.

All of those assumptions were wrong. She was waiting to see what I would bring. Grasping that helped enormously because then I realised that the responsibility to plan was mine, or at least jointly mine. And so it became a matter of priority for me to spend my time between the sessions figuring out how I was going to make best use of the session—not sitting passively by, waiting for the therapist to 'magic' me better. It became a collaborative effort, which in turn reduced the power differential between us. I wasn't in 'child' mode, waiting for the 'grown up' to know what to do, no matter how 'child-like' I felt at times, especially when switched to traumatised parts of myself. I was responsible for my own recovery and so I had to take seriously each week the issue of what I wanted to accomplish and how best I wanted to use the time. I had to see myself as the driver and use the therapist as the navigator. I was deciding where we were going and I was putting my foot down to get us there. The therapist was there to guide me and shout directions. When we worked like this, it was a productive journey.

4.   Respect the 'therapeutic frame'

It's not a phrase that we are taught about in the normal course of events: the 'therapeutic frame'. It's most definitely part of the 'therapy school curriculum' (for at least some schools of thought) but it's an important concept for us as clients to grasp too. It can be thought of as the 'implicit rules' for therapy but some of the rules are explicit too, such as the session times and days. In our culture of CityLink vans and Tesco deliveries, we are used to selecting our 'slot' and then changing it up to 24 hours beforehand if it no longer suits. But therapy doesn't work like that. We need to respect the frame: when it happens, where it happens, how often it happens, how it happens. This isn't a hair appointment that we can rearrange at a moment's notice. It's a good thing that we allow it to be a fixed point in our week, and for everything else to flow around it, because it establishes within us what is important, and perhaps for the first time we value ourselves by valuing our therapy. And it's a good thing that we keep the boundaries of this set-aside time: this is our time to talk in a way that we don't talk the rest of the week. This isn't a social chat, nor a stiff, professional interaction. This is a relational encounter where we have a different set of rules, where it's okay to disclose, where it's okay to be self-focussed, where it's okay for parts to come to the fore, where it's okay to feel and express emotions. But there are a thousand ways that we can sabotage this therapy and attack the frame—we can be late, we can be distracted, we can be sulky, we can fail to pay, we can 'forget' to come, we can attack the therapist, we can leave early, we can refuse to engage, we can pretend to be open, we can mess about and play a role. But none of that will help us to recover. If we respect the frame, we respect ourselves.

5. Encourage others to respect your therapy

At first, before he trained to become a therapist, my husband didn't have a clue what it was all about. He was left at home, literally holding the baby, while I went off to 'do drawings' and 'have a nice a chat'. He simply couldn't imagine what went on in my sessions. During a period of huge stress for both of us, at times he succumbed to thinking that it was all a bit self-indulgent. Fortunately, he loves me and fortunately he is quick and eager to learn and once he began to understand the nature of the work—a 'cosy chat' is as far from reality as possible—he began to be supportive of my need for therapy and he began actively to protect this time too. Not everyone will have such understanding and supporting partners or family and it's a tough battle to have to face, albeit a necessary one. It is vital, where possible, to construct boundaries around your therapy times and to elicit the support of everyone and anyone in doing that. It's hard enough to face your own ambivalence at going back to that scary room with the scary therapist to talk about the scary things… it's even harder if a partner has 'accidentally' stayed late at work and won't be home in time to babysit. Difficult conversations need to take place, a commitment from both of you (including, where old enough, your children) that this is important, that this matters, that it will help, that it's a priority, and that it's okay for you to commit the time to it. Feeling guilty, feeling 'selfish' for taking out this time, doesn't benefit anyone.

6. Do the hardest work between sessions

In our avoidance, how often do we get to the end of a session and sigh with relief that that's over with for another week, and we can put it all out of mind again? It's a helpful tool to be able to segment our experiences like that—to a point. But recovery comes through challenging our habitual avoidance of all things traumatic, in order to resolve them. And contrary to popular belief, that resolution doesn't come in the therapy session alone. If you have a two-hour session, or two one-hour sessions during the week, that still leaves you with 166 hours where you can make progress. So much of the therapeutic work is about changing the wiring of our brains, these neural networks of habits and automatic responses that we have lived with for decades.

The therapy session itself can be a catalyst for that change but new neural networks get laid down through repetition. Saying once in a therapy session, 'It wasn't my fault' will make a difference, but not as much as will saying it a hundred times during the ensuing week. Journalling, thinking, writing, drawing, meditating, considering, dreaming... our brains can be busy and creating new connections all week long. We can do the work of therapy outside the session by implementing what we have discovered in the session, by reinforcing those new truths and realities.

In one Sensorimotor Psychotherapy session, I enjoyed the benefit for the first time of standing up straight, lengthening my spine, and feeling strength and power and competence in my body. It was a striking experience, as my therapist guided me to mindfully notice the different parts of my body and to imagine myself strong and capable. Previously, when I stood up, I felt weak and helpless and panicky. This was a simple exercise and yet it was a breakthrough moment for me. But the real progress was through my reinforcing it dozens of times the following week, by practising 'standing', by doing the exercise over and over and over again. I practised it for weeks and months and years, until I had a habit ingrained in my neural networks, a resource that I could draw on at any moment. I could stand up in front of a room of people—in front of a whole auditorium of people!—and feel strong, and capable and competent. And all because I had taken that initial spark in that one single therapy session and repeated and reinforced it again and again and again until the change was there, in my body, as a memory, as a habit.

The same is true for journalling. Very often I would leave a session with one dominating thought from the session to consider in the following week. 'It wasn't my fault.' There was this magical moment in therapy, this moment of revelation, a peeling away of my worldview and the sneak peek of a new vista. But I had to reinforce it afterwards. So I would go away and journal. I would write reams and reams and reams on whether it was my fault or not, what the arguments for and against were, what it felt like to think it wasn't, what the reality of my innocence made me feel. Thousands of words, thinking it through, considering it, contemplating it, turning it over in my mind. And when I hit a hurdle, when something jarred and would not lie flat and smooth within me, that then became the focus for the following week, and that session would have fresh impetus and direction. Each week, building on the next, by laying foundations and fetching bricks, so that at the start of every session the materials were at hand, the ground was prepared, and I was ready to build.

7.   Honour and guard your relationship with your therapist

It's easy to think of your therapist as a 'professional', where 'professional' means they are not really human, and it's just a job, and they don't really care, and they have no feelings to hurt. Certainly, you're not responsible for your therapist's feelings, and you shouldn't hold back on talking about what you need to, for fear of upsetting them. But they are still a human being. You can't build a relationship of collaboration and mutuality unless you treat them fairly. You expect confidentiality of them but how many times do you slag them off to your friends or undermine them or mock them? How many times does your disdain for them leak out like gravy from a pie? Do you make it hard for them to work with you? Do you turn the therapy into a battle? Are you goading them to reject you?

There may be many understandable reasons—not least your trauma, not least a background of disorganised attachment, not least the stress of your current circumstances—why at times you hate your therapist with passion. But they are just a human being too and, regardless of their efforts to show 'unconditional positive regard', it's so much easier for them to help you if you don't fight them all the way. If you can honour your relationship with them, if you can guard it by treating them with dignity and respect, if you can be quick to apologise and quicker to forgive, you will gain in the end.

I'm not talking about turning a blind eye or being abused by a bad therapist, an unprofessional or an exploitative one. I'm talking about meeting the good one halfway and showing them that you respect them and that you're not out to destroy them. They hold a lot of anxiety much of the time in this work—the anxiety of your self-harm or suicidality, the anxiety of whether they're retraumatising you by going too fast or too slow, the anxiety over whether they've said the right thing or done the right thing… Everyone works better and relates better from a place of safety and one of the first mentalising exercises you can do—without going overboard and taking responsibility for them and worrying about them or caretaking them—is to consider how you are with your therapist, and whether you're making it safe for them to work with you, or whether they're distracted or on edge because of your threats.

Nor can we do the work unless we're willing to relate. We can't hang around at the edges, wearing a mask, saying what we think will please or placate. This is therapy. This is where things get said, feelings get felt, reality is faced. It's not a place for emotional snakes and ladders, playing games with the therapist, trying to avoid saying anything real, trying to hide all emotion, trying to keep one step ahead. That was the way I had to be as a child, to survive. But therapy required that I was willing to engage, that I was willing to be honest—with the therapist and myself—and that I was willing to be challenged. Admittedly, it was something that took me a while to learn. But the therapeutic relationship was something that I had to commit to, to stick with, to be honest about, rather than picking it up and discarding it after a few sessions or months because I didn't feel it was working. Why wasn't it working? What was going on? Had I talked about it? Had I tried to work it through? Some relationships, of course, can't be worked through. But many of them can, and we need to learn how.

8. Don't undermine therapy by contradicting it the rest of the time

We want to live free from abuse, but we continue to abuse ourselves. We want to develop secure attachment, but we continue to be pulled around in insecure-ambivalent relationships. We want to put up boundaries with our abusers, but then we invite them to stay. And we go back into our session the following week, and we hang our head in shame, and we feel the full force of our self-frustration as we say, 'I'm not making any progress.'

I used to think that I would be able to get something sorted in therapy, and that it would spill magically over into 'real' life. I would talk about some trauma, understand what distorted belief it had led me into, and then the 'ping!' moment would magic into being wonderful new behaviours. But eventually I realised that the 'ping!' moment in therapy is often just the start. I had to make active choices to reinforce that by my actions the rest of the week. I had to start choosing not to abuse myself, not to let my abusers near, and to distance myself from people who sought to control and use me. Very often I had to change my behaviours first, whilst still struggling with the concept, before the 'ping!' moment really landed.

But what never worked was pursuing one course of action in therapy, whilst undermining it elsewhere. I didn't want to live in the hyperarousal of attachment insecurity, the up-down, love-hate of borderline relationships. I didn't like how I became around certain people — the pull they had on me, the submission they tricked out of me, the way my mind got fixed on where they were and what they were doing. I tried compromising and tried just talking about it in therapy, without doing anything about it. But of course it didn't work. And it infected my therapeutic relationship, making me nervous and twitchy about that, making me 'see' abandonment when it wasn't there. It affected the work I was trying to achieve. I had to make hard decisions, cut off dead branches, steer clear of the nettles. Anything else would undermine what the sessions were for. There had to be congruence between my intentions in therapy and my actions in the rest of life.

9. Learn

Psychoeducation helps. It really, really helps. At the time of the abuse, did you freeze and do you feel bad now that you didn't do anything to fight back or escape? You need to understand the freeze response. Is your heart pounding and your brain has gone blank and you can't find your words? You need to understand about triggers and the front and back brain. Does your therapist's holiday feel like a threat to your very existence and when she comes back are you both delighted to see her and a ball of rage? You need to understand about disorganised attachment.

So much of the time, we beat ourselves up because we don't understand trauma, we don't understand about dissociation, and we don't understand about attachment. And yet almost all of our behaviours and beliefs are logical in the light of these three subjects. I felt powerless when night after night I couldn't get to sleep because I couldn't seem to calm down. Once I understood about hyperarousal and the sympathetic nervous system, I stopped feeling so bad about it. It didn't instantly solve the insomnia, but it stopped me 'fearing the fear'—the vicious cycle of anxiety that keeps us locked into a fight-or-flight response. Once I understood that dissociation is a normal and natural response to trauma, I stopped feeling that I was such a freak. Once I understood that the out-breath activates the parasympathetic nervous system and helps to regulate our arousal, I began to feel that there was something that I could do to manage my distress.

Often we go into therapy with the expectation that it will be like visiting the hospital or the GP—that the expert, the white coat, will know what they are talking about, and we just have to give blood, or flex our knee, or say 'aaah', and everything will be alright. But therapy isn't like that. The more we understand about dissociation, the more we understand about trauma, the more we understand about attachment, the easier we will find it to understand ourselves. And the more we understand ourselves, the more we will value ourselves as ingenious survivors who are courageous and resourceful, rather than as the screw-ups that we so often think we are. Psychoeducation helps teach us to have self-respect, and it teaches us tools for managing our distress that we didn't learn as we grew up. Sometimes that education comes within a therapy session, from the therapist, but we have 166+ hours a week where we can work on this stuff for ourselves, and keep the sessions for the application of that knowledge. Knowledge is power, and power is what we need to overcome the disempowerment of trauma.

10. Don't let go of the rest of life
It's important to prioritise therapy but it's important to keep it in balance, too. Therapy is there to help you re-engage with life and conquer the world. It's not there as a substitute for life. Don't give

up supportive friendships because now you have therapy; don't quit work because you want to focus exclusively on therapy; don't stop going out and having fun because every night you're journalling for your session. Keep everything in balance, and everything in perspective. You don't want to spend five years in therapy, and then at the end of it look up and realise that you've lost the life you've been trying to build. It's good to keep focused on the work that you're doing in therapy, but don't become so problem-saturated that there's no outlet for your steam. The things that you work through in therapy need to be worked out in real life; therapy is where you get to practice and figure out your relating, but you need real relationships in real life to put it into action.

Therapy is our springboard for life. It's important that we use it to launch ourselves into real living. Sometimes our therapy becomes all we have, because our lives are so deprived. But then it is through therapy that we must increase our relational and experiential wealth, because therapy won't last forever and it's only a poor imitation of the rich life that we have ahead of us.

CHAPTER FOURTEEN

The Body Remembers

I hate my body. It was there, always there, during the abuse. My mind went away but my body could not. My mind could forget. We parcelled up little chunks of our mind, bit by bit and sent them off into dim little rooms where they could be forgotten and not heard. We didn't want to watch, we didn't want to see. But our body was there.

Our body remembers. It always remembers, and it doesn't lie. Sometimes our mind looks on and we're at war—always at war sometimes it seems—our body reacting like it can remember what our mind cannot. It pulls away, it arches, it hurts, it screams, it recoils, it goes limp, it aches with tiredness, it refuses to settle, refuses to sleep. It's confusing. Sometimes, our mind can't remember anything. 'Why is our body reacting?' we think. Because our body hasn't forgotten. It's learnt to react and it just keeps on reacting. We've trained our mind not to react, to look away, to pretend we weren't there, to pretend we don't know. But our body doesn't lie.

Sometimes our body talks to us. It tries to tell us stuff we don't want to hear. Our body remembers what we cannot. It shouts about it, clamours to be heard. Our mind won't listen, it won't hear it. So our body hurts. Really hurts. Sometimes the pain is so bad, our mind wants to go mad. Literally mad. Anything but feel that pain. Our body shouts, shouts, shouts *It hurts, it hurt!* It can't have hurt, says our mind, because nothing happened. But our body doesn't lie.

Every day our body hurts, every day it's too-tired. Too-too-tired. *Why is it so tired?* thinks our mind. It's got nothing to be tired about. It's tired about a long time ago. It was so tired then, yanked out of bed, taken out, nasty things, nasty nasty things at night. It hurt, it hurt. Now again the body is telling us, it hurt. When they hurt us with knives, our mind wasn't there. It couldn't be there. But the body was there and it wants us to know. We don't want to know. So we're always at war.

Then if we don't listen the body tells us again. Again and again. Pain, chronic pain, chronic awful unbearable pain. Every day. And smells, smells that can't be there, sounds we can hear but we know can't be there, that feeling, that weird yukky awful feeling on our skin, and our whole body cold and cold and colder even though we can't be that cold. We can't be that cold. The thermometer says it's 28 degrees in here. We can't be that cold. But the body is remembering, and it's telling us that we were cold. And our body doesn't lie. It doesn't know how to lie. It just tells us how it is, how it was.

Our mind isn't very good sometimes at telling what's what. What was then, what is now—all a muddle, such a muddle. Our body breathes too fast, our heart going pitter-patter-pitter-patter too-too-fast. Sick feelings in our tummy, numbness in our fingertips, wet feelings where we don't want wet feelings. Our mind doesn't understand. Maybe there's something wrong with us, maybe we're poorly. Maybe we're not. Our body doesn't lie. It's just remembering.

It remembers the pain as bad as it was then. Sometimes we cry, sometimes we scream, sometimes we pass out because the pain just hurts so bad. But there isn't a knife now, no-one's hurting us now, there's no blood now. It can't be hurting this much. Our body is just remembering. Then slowly, bit by bit, slowly-too-slowly, our mind remembers too. Horrible things to remember. Heart-hurting, brain-searing horrible things to remember. But when we remember, when we say it, when we tell it, then suddenly our body stops remembering. All of a sudden, like a dam has burst. All of a sudden it stops shouting at us, because we've listened. Our body doesn't lie. It's just remembering. I'm trying not to hate my body.

CHAPTER FIFTEEN

Suicide: to be or not to be

I could cope with it no longer. Every part of me—eyelids, throat, bowels—everything was clenched tight in a ball of furious unbearability. This feeling—such a feeling!—loomed up over me like some prehistoric sea-monster, ready to snap me up and devour me, ready to pilfer my bones and pick apart my brain. This feeling was too much. It was all too much. Feelings weren't supposed to be this overwhelming. I didn't know how to 'do' feelings. I didn't know you could feel like this. I certainly didn't know you could survive feeling like this. And so all that I wanted, all that I could see, the only option in this fetid slime-pit of despair, was suicide.

If you've never felt suicidal, never stood at the abyss and swayed unsteadily forwards, ready to fall, ready to go, you won't really know what I'm talking about. I'm sure everyone, from time to time, momentarily ponders the possibility of death: the lazy, languid option of two steps to the left and into the traffic. But not this.

Not this heaving, terrifying, sickening overload of emotion that will crush you if you don't act. Not this sense that if you don't kill yourself soon, you will be tortured to death by your own emotion. Not this deep-in-your-bones conviction that your very life is a reek and a stench and your best service to humanity is to rid it of you. That's the kind of suicidal ideation I'm talking about. The kind that hurts too much not to obey.

The first time I felt like that, I was at University and I was twenty years old. Over several difficult weeks at the beginning of my second year, a dark, oppressive cloud had rolled in over the fens, into my bones, and down into my guts. Everywhere I went, everything I felt, was this dank, gloomy cloud, robbing me of hope, robbing me of joy. I now know that it's called 'depression', but this was the 90s — before anyone decided that it was 'good to talk' about mental health. Depression meant you were just a bit down, a bit can't-be-bothered, a bit low. I didn't know that depression is a parasite that sucks the life out of you. I didn't know that it bleaches colours from your vision, that it leaches tastes from your food, that it plugs closed every orifice in your mind where joy or pleasure or contentment might enter. It starves you from the inside.

This depression robbed me of daylight, and in rolled the thunderclouds, the lightning strikes of pain. Memories long suppressed—memories long dissociated—clapped out of the heavens and set me ablaze. Sudden, intrusive, bewildering images of something I couldn't quite see, but which I would now label as abuse. But it was in my body that I felt it. The lightning strike of a flashback lit up my being with indescribable, tormenting pain. I had to get away from it, but I didn't know how. Night after night, day after day, my body convulsed with the agony of unremembered trauma. I felt I was going mad. After six shameful weeks, backlogged on my course, isolated from support, disgusted with myself for this outbreak of 'insanity', I could bear it no longer. In the damp chill of a November night, in the jaundiced flicker of my student bedside lamp, I lined up the paracetamol and decided that I would fight it no longer.

That was twenty years ago, and yet here I am today. There have been many other nights like that. But I'm still here. It's a few years now since my last serious attempt. So the fact that I'm still alive—does that mean that I wasn't serious, that I was just pretending, that I was just doing it for attention, that it was just a phase, that I never really intended it? Not at all. For me, suicide was never the choice I wanted to make. Rather, it was the choice I didn't feel I could avoid.

Suicidal feelings are intensely painful. They are the unbearability of despair, inarticulate and visceral. They compel you to act. They drive you to leap and run and squeal and flee, like a cat falling into a fire. They are not about feeling 'down'. They are about feeling that there is no end to the feelings, and that you can bear it no longer. And then comes the stillness. In the maelstrom of agony is the choice—that breathless, final choice that you're going to end it, and you can do it, and you have to do it, and so now you will. And, addictive as crack, then comes the feeling of calm, because it's over, and it's going to be over, and you're not going to have to fight it any longer. It's the most dangerous time. When a suicide is 'completed', people often talk about how the person seemed 'ok' beforehand, the last time they saw them—sometimes 'upbeat', 'better', 'calm' even. But it was the swoon before the suicide.

And it scared me. Whenever I reached that point, whenever it went still within myself, with the voices quiet and the emotions numb, I was terrified rather than soothed. I felt annihilated. Always, for me, at those moments, somehow a swooping, powerful, unremitting sense of purpose has taken hold of me and propelled me back into life. Something has dawned. I have needed to live, and make a difference, more than I've needed to die. But an ugly battle always prefaces that shift and I have not always survived it unscathed...

Being dissociative, with disconnections and contradictions inherent within my mind, sometimes one part of me overdoses and then another—usually a part we called 'Flag'—sounds the alarm and mobilises us to survive. It is an ambivalence that appears to the uninitiated like attention-seeking, but the reality is more subtle and complex. It is the inevitable consequence of a dissociative mind where my actions are not linked with my intentions or memories. I am fortunate not to have died. I am fortunate that my organs have not been damaged. It's not a course of action I would recommend to anyone. It's a course of action that I would do everything in my power to stop another person taking. But it's a course of action all too common for survivors of trauma.

Bethany Brand (2001) estimated that suicidal ideation afflicts 61 to 72% of dissociative survivors. 1-2% of people with DID have completed suicide. So I am not alone, and nor are the hundreds of other dissociative survivors who have been in touch with PODS over the last few years who also live lives of quiet desperation, teetering on the edge of the abyss. In 2011 my husband Rob wrote an article entitled 'Don't do it: a partner's experience of self-harm and suicidality' (available at www.pods-online.org.uk) because he eventually understood that he is not alone, and he wanted other partners to know that there they are not alone either, and that there is hope. Things do get better, although often not before they have gotten worse.

There were different reasons at different times for my suicidality. Mostly, it was because it seemed to offer a way out, to end the pain. Sometimes, it was the fabled 'cry for help'. I have never understood people's negativity about this. When you're feeling extreme distress, when things hurt so badly that you are contemplating the ultimate cure, why shouldn't you cry for help? It's natural. And when you don't know how to put what you're feeling into words, when you don't know how to elicit support from others—or no one is listening and you can't get the help you need—then a 'cry for help' is a natural thing. Only rarely for me was it a naked, all-out cry for help—like many people with avoidant attachment, I tend to withdraw when I am in pain, and seek solitude rather than the care and support of others. But with my attachment style aside, a cry for help seems an eminently sensible, survival-based option to take.

At other times, suicidal ideation has been a way of taking control. When everything else around me has felt out-of-control—my feelings, my behaviours, others' behaviour towards me, my circumstances, my finances, my flashbacks, my body—then suicide at least gave me a semblance of control. Sometimes, the planning of it would bring comfort, a way for me to order my world and feel that I had choices and things that I could do, in contrast to the powerlessness and overwhelm of what else I was experiencing. It was an outlet for my rage, this torrent of self-destructiveness at all the injustice and all the pain and all the horror of all the criminality that had ever been visited upon me. Sometimes it was an eruption of shame and self-loathing and a despicable, end-it-all explosion of fury that they had wanted me dead, back then when I was child, so I would give them what they wanted now, as an adult, because now I have the power. That kind of rage often finds no other place to land.

Suicidal thoughts were also a natural consequence of the despair that so dominated me. I was unable to visualise a future. What was the point in living if there was nothing beyond the torment of my memories, my wretched self-loathing, my isolation, my poverty? In the really difficult times, when every night was bereft of sleep and flooded with memories of torture, when the daytimes were a muddle of switching and fugues and anxiety and nausea, what was the point of living? I couldn't imagine things getting any better. There was nothing that I enjoyed. No one understood. I felt marooned, alone, isolated, outcast. I couldn't reach people, and they couldn't reach me. I couldn't 'change' quickly enough. I was seen as 'problematic' and 'difficult' and 'challenging' and 'bad'. I was told that I was choosing to be the way I was. I was labelled, and judged, and condemned. So what was the point? If I was intrinsically bad, as so many people at that time seemed to believe, then where was my future? I could people-watch in Costa and feel like some persecuted illegal immigrant. How on earth could I fit in? How could I be what I needed to be, in order to be what was acceptable to be? To be or not to be—that then was the question.

Suicide made sense, whilst living did not. What I didn't realise at the time was that I was wearing a blindfold. So while well-meaning people were telling me that 'It's not all bad' and 'Things will get better' and 'It's time to move on', I couldn't see what they were talking about. When people talked about having a hope and a future, I didn't know what they meant. Under my blindfold, all I saw was the blackness. All I could hear was the silence. There was no future that I could see. There was no laughter, no joy, no hope, no potential 'acts of triumph'. My current experience was all that I had, and I lived it under the strictures of a blindfold. So I didn't believe people. I thought reality was all that I could see. I discounted their vision.

And that is where faith came in: not faith in the sense of organised religion, but faith as an inchoate reaching out for what isn't, and willing it, believing it, to be. Faith is being certain of what we cannot see. Faith is saying that there will be a beautiful sunset, even though it's not yet dawn. Faith is that experience of flying above the gloom-roll of clouds and saying, 'It's a beautiful day and the sun is shining'. And when I didn't have faith for myself, which for several years was most days, it was important that someone else had it for me. More often than not, my therapists and my husband held my faith for me. They kept saying, 'The sun is still shining, even though you can't see it today.' And I would argue with them that they were wrong, and I was right, but in the end they won. They won, not through the brute force of shouting at me and making me see, but simply because they just kept saying it. What they had was a memory of the sun shining, even though it was a gloomy day. And one of the things that began to change for me was that I began to learn to be mindful. I began to be able to notice—'Just notice! Just be curious!' as my therapist would say in that sing-song voice. I began to notice that the sun was shining, on days that it was. Even if only for a moment, it was important to direct my attention to it, to catch that ray, to focus on it, to make my brain imprint it in my memory, so that in the future I could look back and remember that it had been there. So much of faith is built on memory. When we're struggling, we can't remember a single sunny day. I had to retrain my brain to notice the sun was shining so that I could remember in the future that it would shine again, even on the most dismal of days.

And I began to notice that feelings come as a wave, that they crest, and that then they fall. Too often, on the crest, in the unbearability of emotion, I wanted to die. I couldn't see that if I could just ride it, if I could just surf along under its frothing underhang, things would feel better, and other options would open up to me. Because it didn't feel like it would feel any better. We can only feel right-here-right-now feelings. We can't feel a feeling from the future. So we have to know, or imagine, or believe that we're going to feel better later. And that's hard. We have to remember that when we felt like this before, that feeling didn't last. I developed two mantras: 'Feelings are meant to be felt' (which as a consequence means that feelings don't have be acted upon—just felt), and 'Feelings don't last forever.' Everything screamed at me that pain, this suffering-screech of unbearable despair, would remain until I did something about it, and the only thing I could do about it was to kill myself.

But then I learned that there are things that we can do when we feel big feelings: things that don't involve suicide, nor even self-harm.

Things that are soothing. At first, I wanted just to vomit even at the sound of the words 'self-soothing'. There was something distinctly, creepily uncomfortable about them, like somehow it was to do with abuse (it's not) or that it's selfish (it's not) or that it shows that I'm not coping (it doesn't). I had to learn that self-soothing is merely a set of strategies we can have for helping our emotions to remain within a 'window of tolerance' — not too high, not too low. It's things we can do that help us rebalance, like playing Sudoku; or talking to a friend; or watching comfort telly; or going for a walk; or filing and tidying; or sleeping; or counting backwards; or taking a shower; or cleaning; or shredding old bank statements; or breathing from the belly; or journalling; or birdwatching; or anything at all that helps or distracts or amuses or reassures. Because right at that moment, on that wave of crushing emotion, too often I would freeze and forget that there are things that I can do (other than suicide) that will make things just a teeny bit more bearable, just get me through the next five minutes, just get me acting and being and asserting my right to life, rather than being drowned under the collapsing wave of too-much-too-much.

I personally found it helpful when people heard my distress but didn't overreact to it: when they didn't swing, full-scale into 'call 999, call an ambulance, call a doctor, call a priest'. When they heard how terrible it was for me, and they just sat there with me and went 'ouch', rather than ramping up my anxiety by talking of Places of Safety and sections and assessments. And I know it was hard for other people, as I sit now on the other side and have people tell me just how desperate and despairing and futile and empty they feel. I want to swing into action, and make sure they're safe, and pass the hot potato of responsibility and risk onto someone else. I don't want to be the person who fails to act, who fails to do something, and finds them dead the next day. The anxiety of that is horrific.

So I see it on both sides now, and know that sometimes the right thing to do is to swing into action, and protect people from themselves. But mostly there's a space before we get to that point, a gap in the road from the kerb to the pavement, where we just need to step across rather than falling down into something we can't get ourselves out of. It's the gap where we can just sit with the person, and hear them, and soothe their emotions with them, and once they have settled, in a very clear way but in a very unpressured way, tell them quietly that the sun is still shining above the clouds but we know they can't see it right now.

I've always been amazed at how, when I've been at my most distraught, the simplest things have had the biggest effect. When I'm on the other side of it, I assume that there is nothing I can say to another suicidal person that will make any difference. But when I've been on the edge of the abyss, simple words have made a world of difference to me. Just telling me to hold on has been immeasurably powerful. Reminding me of one good thing in my future has made that one thing loom slightly larger in my mind, and I'm grateful, because I'd forgotten it. When I'm feeling that there is no place for me on earth, that I don't belong, that I have no purpose, that I make no difference, that there's no point, then just hearing someone say, 'You matter, and there is only one you' can change everything, even if it's only for a minute. The effect is amplified if it's from someone who genuinely cares. When we're starving, sometimes even crumbs can make us feel less hungry. I've always thought, in reference to other people, that I should never forget that when I've been desperate, it makes a difference when someone hears my pain, and it makes a difference when someone reminds me too that the pain won't last forever.

This isn't meant as a glib, easy-cook response to suicide, and nor is this meant to be a comprehensive catalogue of the whys and why nots, the things to say and the things not to do. Some people do kill themselves, no matter what anyone else has said, no matter how sunny it was going to be the next day. Sometimes we can't pull back from the edge. It would be better—so, so much better—if events and circumstances and trauma and abuse and emotions and damage and pressure didn't push us right to the edge. When people say that suicide is selfish, they fail to understand that what is truly selfish is the abuse and the pressure that was put on that person, to make them feel so desperate and hopeless and ostracised and alone that they chose instead to die. Suicide offers an escape to unbearable suffering. Maybe if there wasn't that suffering in the first place, maybe if we'd been helped more to bear it, maybe if the world wasn't the way it was and there were never any clouds, we wouldn't have to jump. I'm hoping, praying, pleading that no one jumps. Suicide is not the answer, although I know how much at times it feels as if it must be. I'm glad—now—that I didn't kill myself. And why didn't I? Maybe because I am one of the lucky unlucky ones—unlucky enough to have been abused, but lucky enough to have some support now, as an adult, to work it through.

The best response we can have to suicidal people is to support them way before they get to that point, which in times of mental health cuts and austerity measures is easier said than done. But we can still try. I found a purpose in life, of recovery being my best revenge and a deep-in-my-guts need to bring change to this world, as my reason to push through the pain and to keep on living. It's what gets me out of bed every day of the week: the need to be alive, so that I can change something, and make things better, even if only a little. Judith Lewis Herman talked about a survivor mission being a crucial part of recovery.

We have to find better reasons to live than all our reasons to die. That's why I don't like suicide websites, and internet forums which focus only on the negative. I don't need to be pulled down even lower when I'm already on the floor. I need to look up, and I need other people to help me look up. Empathy is important, but hope is more so. I'm glad I kept on hoping when everything seemed so hopeless. Because recovery is possible, and I could never have imagined back then, when I was twenty, with the paracetamol lined up and the hopelessness of despair beckoning me downwards, that life could be as hopeful and fruitful and positive and blessed as it is for me now. There is hope.

CHAPTER SIXTEEN

A grief ago

Why hadn't the world noticed? That was the thought that kept haunting me. *Why hasn't anyone seen?* I knew with my rational mind that no one else knew, that all that had happened was that I had spoken, in a room with a counsellor, about an event from long ago. No one else had been listening; no one else had heard. And yet somehow, coming to the realisation myself that my baby had been killed, feeling the pain of unadmitted grief, what shocked me was that no one else knew. The world just went on as it did before. No one knew, or no one said they knew. I came out of that session, with tears clogged up like blades in my throat. I wanted to shout and to scream with the pain of it all. I wanted my unfurled rage to light up the sky, to glimmer on the rooftops, to announce this most tragic of events. I wanted to tell everyone I met, because it was all that was in my mind. This awful thing has happened. I have to tell someone. I have to let them know. My grief needs an outlet.

But there was no one to tell, and the world walked on as if nothing had happened. And yet how many people did I pass on the High Street that day, who had their own unexpressed grief writ large on their hearts and small on their faces? Maybe they passed by and thought me unkind for not stopping them, saying how sorry I was, and holding their pain on my face. I didn't know their untold tragedies, and they didn't know mine. That is just the way the world is. Our grief is silent and invisible.

I heard of an African village where, when someone dies, the whole village changes something—on the outside of their house, in their gardens. The next morning, the bereaved can see that their world has changed, and it is acknowledged by all. That was what I struggled with: everything seemed to have changed, my world upside down, but everyone's gardens and houses looked the same.

As an adult, married, we tried for many years to have children. I had three early miscarriages, but no viable pregnancy. It hurt. It was another loss, more silent grief. It rearranged the way I viewed the world. I realised that the path I'd taken for granted—meet someone, get married, settle down, have children—is an illusion. What happens to 'lots' of people doesn't always happen to me. It's a fantasy, rubbed raw away by the vagaries of reality. Things don't work out the way we want them to, and it's painful. *Pain is inevitable; suffering is optional,* I read somewhere. I didn't know what that meant. I felt blamed by it for my suffering. I felt that someone was wiping away my experience, saying it didn't matter, saying that I shouldn't mind. But I did mind. I minded very much that I gave fifteen years of my adult life to caring for other people's babies, but I wasn't 'allowed' my own. I wasn't quite sure who I was blaming for it. I wasn't quite sure who I thought was in charge of these 'rules', that disqualified me from being a parent, from having a family, from being a mother. Wasn't it enough that I'd been abused in childhood, lost two babies at 12 and 14, the products of rape, the victims of murder? I wanted to rail against the injustice of the world, as if my railing would make it somehow different, as if my protest would change the reality. It didn't.

I was a foster carer to twenty-two children. I loved those kids. One we had long-term, for ten years, until Children's Services in their wisdom decided to move her to another family and rehabilitate her to her mum. Everything fell apart. She left suddenly, in disputed circumstances, all of us disagreeing about the best way forwards to meet her complex needs, the damage from a too-terrible infancy. And then she was gone. Ten years of tucking her in at night, telling her that I loved her to the moon and back. Ten years of wishing the best for her, pushing against the stagnant cesspit of policies and procedures to try to improve her world. And no more. We had been halfway to adoption with her, counted her as our daughter, and then she was gone. It wrenched something out of my soul.

On the day my father died, I received a text to tell me that he had passed away at eight o'clock that morning. That was all. It was from an aunt, who reached out through the forbidden distance between me and my family, first to tell me that he was dying, and afterwards to recount to me his last few days. She knew she was taking a risk by telling me: risk of expulsion from the clan, tightly knit together against me. On phoning the hospital, I was told there was only one daughter, my sister, and that she was currently with him. On the obituary it said that my father had been a loving husband to his wife, and a beloved father of my sister: there was no mention of me. As in Orwell's 1984 I was expunged from the record. My crime was to have been abused, and not to have kept it silent.

I grieved my Dad. So much had been so evidently wrong in my childhood. After rape and murder and torture, it's hard to look back and see the good things, but there were some, and all of them involved my Dad. He played football with me: in the garden, in the park, in the street. I watched him play golf, cricket, tennis, squash. We shared a love of driving; he taught me to look in the distance, not at the bonnet, to change gear before the bend, not on it, to watch the camber on a corner and see where the rainwater pools. But when I told him I'd been abused, he cut me out rather than drawing me in. You assume that blood is thicker than water, that family will always be there for you (even the bad ones), until you realise that there are some things that won't be tolerated, and in some families, speaking about abuse is the unforgiveable sin.

I hadn't seen him for seven years when he died. I was scared of him, right up until the moment that he died. But still I grieved him. I worked hard at the grief process: I journalled, day and night, thousands upon thousands of words scribbled fast and hard, good emotions, hard emotions, stuck-in the-middle-of-nowhere emotions. I burrowed around until I had a name for that feeling, until I knew why I was crying. There was so much that I didn't understand. He was the only father I'd had, and now he was gone, and at the funeral many must have wondered why I wasn't there, and what kind of daughter wouldn't come to her pay her respects to her own father. *One that wasn't welcome,* I wanted to say, in the imaginary conversation in my head. The reality was that I didn't know what people would say and think, because I didn't know what they had been told. I couldn't *imagine* what they might have been told. 'She said she was abused and so we disowned her'? Why would parents do that? But I continued to need him to be innocent, even after his death.

Grieving is a strange thing. I hadn't realised how physically exhausting it can be. I wanted my grief to be just 'in my head' — safely contained, manageable. I didn't realise that grief pervades your whole body. It is your body that grieves. Three months after he died, I was training, and suddenly in the audience I saw him. My heart slammed in my chest, *thud-thud,* a great heaving, heavy *thud.* I shifted back and to the left, blinked hard, looked away, looked back, and he was gone. An hour or so later, it happened again. I was able to catch the panic as it rose bilious within me, telling myself, *It's just my brain trying to pattern-match. My brain has never known my Dad dead. It's playing catch-up.*

For months he visited me nightly in my dreams. They were not good dreams. I saw him again at other times. *My brain is playing catch-up,* I said to myself a hundred times a day, *I'm not going mad.* But it makes you feel insane. Emotions that surge out of nothingness and explode in your chest — *I'm not going mad,* I insisted. Achey, stretched-out, string-like longings like wisps of smoke. I didn't know what I was feeling; I didn't know why I was upset. A lot of the time, all I felt was a simmering rage. *I'm not supposed to be feeling this,* I would say to myself before I had a chance to stop it. *I can feel whatever I'm feeling,* I'd reassure myself sternly in this churned-up stupidity of confusion. *Why am I grieving for a father who rejected me?* I would go around and around — had I been 'rejected', or was it what I deserved? I wanted him to be a good dad and a bad dad all at the same time. And he was dead.

But there was nothing to show for it. I wasn't suddenly busy, arranging a funeral. I didn't receive flowers, or cards of sympathy. It was as if it hadn't happened, just like when my baby died. Is grief then this hidden thing, this shameful thing, this non-event? I was tangled up inside myself at the silence of this situation. Am I not allowed to grieve? Am I not allowed to feel? Am I not the same as other people, who grieve their parents, and other people see it, and know that it's happened, and come to the funeral? I felt in a nether-world of grey, insipid unallowedness.

Barely months after my father died, my husband began an affair. I didn't know it at the time, at least not explicitly. A year later, when I found out, divorce became the next loss. I would have worked things through, mended the breach, tied back together the severed strings of love that had entwined us for fifteen years, but wounded by his own childhood trauma, my husband could not commit and remain faithful to me and me alone. He thought only of himself and shrugged away our relationship as if it had never been. I knew that it wasn't anything to do with me, and he readily agreed: it was about him, his needs, his lostness within himself, his inability to be the man he could have been. He wanted something that only men could give him, so I had to let him go. There was no funeral for that one either.

The grief pulsed hot and cold, with rage, with sadness, with a deep, aching loss. I bundled around myself my close friends, my real friends, found my feet in a different kind of 'family', and determined to establish a new life. *Unless a grain of wheat falls into the earth and dies, it remains alone; but if it dies, it bears much fruit.* In the pain of loss and rejection and betrayal and death, I forced myself to start building a new life, growing some new fruit. *Just start planting*, I kept saying, even though I couldn't see what was ahead. *Just make a start.* Every day I started again. *Don't go down the self-pity route*, became my mantra. I cried, loudly and often, to feel the pain, to lance it, not to slide into despair. I determined not to dissociate it. *Feelings are meant to be felt.* Ten years of learning how to deal with trauma, how to manage distress, fed me lifelines one at a time. *Feelings will pass.* I knew what I knew about the 'stance towards the self', that it's how we feel about ourselves as a result of what happens to us that is critical, not what happens to us. I dug deeper and deeper into foundational beliefs. *It's not about me; it's about them.* Deep breaths. *Bad things happen, but not because of me.*

I learned that self-pity is different to self-compassion, and that the first leads to death but that the second leads to life. I knew I needed to look after myself. I couldn't afford to beat myself up. I began to understand, inch by inch, what it means: *Pain is inevitable, but suffering is optional.* There was nothing I could do to stop the pain: of the abuse, of my babies, of my daughter, of my father, of my husband. All of them involved pain. But I didn't have to amplify it by hating myself for it. That was the suffering that was optional. I didn't have to see myself as broken, unwanted, unworthy, depraved. *Other people's sin is other people's sin,* I kept saying to myself. *I am not contaminated by it.*

I was enticed by the easy way out, of hurting myself rather than feeling the pain. But grieving is feeling the pain. Grieving is seeing just how much it hurts you. Grieving is rocking the ache to sleep inside you, not ripping your guts to shreds to make it go away. Grieving is saying that the pain is what the pain is, not numbing it or dissociating it or inflicting it on others. Grieving is the soul-burning ouch of acceptance that what is lost is lost, what is gone is gone, and only the pain may remain, but I am alive.

A grief ago, I didn't know how to grieve. A husband ago, I thought that marriage was for life. A father ago, I thought that parents are forever. A child ago, I thought that love would conquer all. So many of these griefs, no one noticed. They just ached alone within me. And I didn't ask for any of it. I can't fight it. I can't stop it coming. I can't make it go away. All I can do is let it shape me, where recovery becomes my best revenge, where I become the person I want to be, in spite of the grief, in spite of the pain. All I can do is let it drive me towards the light.

A grief ago, I didn't know how to grieve. But now, my grief has an outlet and it doesn't matter if no one knows.

CHAPTER SEVENTEEN

Ten roadblocks to recovery

1. Believing that recovery isn't possible

'Recovery is impossible. Even the use of the term 'recovery' is cruel, taunting people who cannot recover with the false hope that it is, and shaming them in the process.' So said a fellow delegate at a recent conference, enraged at PODS' tagline: 'making recovery from dissociative disorders a reality.' And I used to agree with him. Everything I had ever previously known about 'mental illness'— erroneously—was that it was incurable and progressive. It was a revelation for me to read the century-old writings about 'dementia praecox', later labelled 'schizophrenia', that gave birth to this misinformed orthodoxy. It took me even longer to separate out 'mental illness' from 'mental distress' and realise that my symptoms were post-traumatic in nature and simply the clamourings of unhealed suffering. It took me longer still to realise that our brains and our bodies are designed to heal, and that we can co-operate with that process.

It was Janina Fisher, amongst others, who opened my eyes. Referring to the survivor of trauma, she wrote: '…if she had the ability as a small child to survive these terrible experiences, then she has all she needs to recover from the symptoms of those experiences.' It helped change my perspective of myself, from a defenceless victim, powerless, devoid of resistance, to a resourceful survivor, courageous and persistent. We survived the real thing, unremitting trauma itself, when we were children. So surely now as adults, with support, we can survive its aftershocks. I began to believe in recovery firstly because I understood the logic of it, and secondly because I began to experience it myself. I began to understand recovery, not as a 'treatment' that is done to us, but as an orientation of my heart, as something that I can take hold of, because I'm powerless no longer. Recovery is possible, but only if we believe it to be so.

2. Believing that I am mentally ill and 'crazy'

To suggest that DID is a mental illness is to suggest that something has gone wrong in the brain, that some form of medicine may be needed to treat it, that this 'illness' may recur, and that it may even be contagious. Likening mental distress to physical illness is inadequate because it pathologises our normal, human suffering and places it squarely in the medical model, at the whim of doctors and 'experts' who can label our experiences as abnormal. I came to realise—eventually—that nothing had gone wrong with my brain: my brain did good. It helped me survive the unendurable by switching off, by limiting my awareness, by refusing to join up as a whole what is too much for a child's brain to bear.

I came to realise that my brain isn't sick. It's what happened to me that was sick—and arguably the people who did what they did to me. My brain just reacted in the best way it could to keep me alive, and to keep me sane. DID is an adaptation to an abusive or traumatic environment. But once that environment changed—once, as an adult, I became safe—I needed to set about the process of re-adapting my brain to a different environment, one where it didn't need to be so focused on threat and trauma and pain. That is the process of recovery, to mould my brain to a new, non-traumatic environment, not to mend it from dysfunction or cure it from illness. My brain had to learn to focus anew on exploration and relationships and joy. Dissociation was logical when I was a child in an unsafe environment. It only became illogical when I persisted in it as an adult in safe surroundings.

3.   Disempowerment by the recovery process

My life is my own now. I am an autonomous human being—an adult—with the right to make choices and decisions about my own life. But that belief was a long time coming. As a child I had few, if any, choices, and abuse stripped me of my free will. Recovery has involved becoming the adult I am, and gaining my freedom to act as I want to: a victim no longer, but a survivor with self-agency.

In this process of recovery, therefore, it was paramount that I was not disempowered by the very people and institutions that were meant to be helping me. Am I given choice, or are my choices made for me? Am I disempowered by an 'expert', someone with all the knowledge and all the power, who doles out a 'treatment' to me that I don't even understand? Or am I empowered by a skilled but humble human being, coming alongside me, not one over me but with me, on a level?

I have been extremely fortunate in the people who have helped me. They have empowered me to discover my own agency, my own ability to act, to find my own identity and forge my own destiny. They have insisted that I sit in the driver's seat: they have held the map, and only occasionally pulled the emergency brake. Had I been disempowered by 'experts', I might not have learned that I am in charge of my own recovery, and that my life is my own to choose now.

4.   Making excuses or bad behaviour

All of us want to behave badly, at least some of the time. After a lifetime of neglect, of not being noticed, of pain going unsoothed, it is a powerful thing to receive comfort and attention and care. We start to discover the unspent rage within us, the greedy grabbing entitlement that says that the world owes us, because of what happened to us. It's hard to blame our abusers, so mostly we blame ourselves. But then we begin to blame others—our GP, our counsellor, our partner, our friend. We hold them culpable for the acts of others, events from years ago. We unleash our outrage, behaving badly, and then we justify it with, 'It wasn't me... I don't remember... It's not my fault... I can't help it.'

But recovery is not recovery if we assume the role of the perpetrator. Recovery demands that we take responsibility for the behaviour of all the different aspects and parts of ourselves. It was an easy-out for me to let my 'Dark' part smoulder and growl; it was expedient to let my teenage parts seethe with adolescent angst. It was harder to accept that their behaviour was mine too, and that by connecting in to these disowned parts of me I was going to have to acknowledge that I wasn't always the person I wanted to be. But this is recovery too: becoming more than our symptoms, our struggles—becoming who at core we aspire to be. Recovery is about becoming whole as a human being, the best human being we can be, and not using our suffering as an excuse to impose suffering on others.

5. Viewing triggers as gremlins, not guides

Triggers came unbidden, unwarned, unwanted: and suddenly *bam!* I was triggered. Before conscious thought had chance to intervene, my body engaged in a fight-flight-freeze response. Back came the terror, the powerlessness, the rage: the visceral memory of childhood trauma. It was terrifying to endure, but eventually I learned that triggers are not a sign, as I so desperately feared, that I was mad. Triggers are merely signposts to what has yet to be integrated in my memory and experience. They are a conditioned response meant to help me, to keep me safe, to avoid something that caused me harm in the past.

But our survival-based back brains aren't smart—they generalise, they extrapolate, they guess: preferring to err on the safe side, they identify a superfluous detail, like 'beard', as a signal of impending threat. Our back brains can't deduce (yet) that lots of men have beards, and that beardedness is not a good predictor of abuse. So it screams a warning at us now, until our front brains can assimilate new data from our now-safe environment, where beardedness is simply a personal grooming preference that speaks nothing of the motivation to perpetrate: like the colour red, or the sound of footsteps, or the odour of sweat, or the feeling of cold.

But triggers came with such overpowering affect, an echo of the feelings I had at the time. So I avoided them at all costs. It took a long time for me to recognise that by doing so I was ignoring their vital message. Triggers are clues about what is still dissociated. I used to complain often that I couldn't remember what happened to me, but then I discounted the hints, stored in procedural, implicit memory, that triggers offered me. Recovery involved accepting triggers as messengers, and learning to listen to the message that they brought, rather than building a life of distraction and noise.

6. Believing that I am a victim

When I was young, I was overwhelmed by trauma so huge that my brain couldn't deal with it. I was a child then—of course I couldn't deal with it. But trauma has a tendency to freeze in place the self-perceptions we held at the time, and many of us struggle to update our 'mental maps', our 'internal working models', with the new information that tells us that we are children no longer, that we are overwhelmed no longer, and that we can and must now make decisions to act.

Slowly it began to dawn on me that recovery would remain forever out of reach if I continued to see myself as a victim, or as a child, overwhelmed and powerless. I had to teach my brain instead that things are different now, that new resources are available, that 'it's not happening now'. I had to see myself not as a powerless, pathetic victim (urgent and primeval though that belief was), but as a resourceful, resilient survivor. It didn't come naturally at all: I had to work at it. I couldn't choose what happened to me as a child, but I could choose how I viewed myself now as an adult who survived that.

Later I learned about Attachment Theory, which teaches us that 'the stance of the self towards experience' (Main, 1991) is paramount, that it's not what happened to us that dictates our destiny so much as how we view ourselves. And I began to realise that recovery was tantalisingly near: because if it is rooted in how I view myself and my experiences, rather than the experiences themselves, then I have some power over it. No one can dictate to me how I should think about myself (although many still try): it's entirely up to me. I am who I believe I am: spirited survivor, not voiceless victim. And that is the very basis of recovery.

7. Believing we're the sum of our symptoms

The experience of DID has been at all times both strange and overpowering. I experience blanks throughout my day— 'microamnesias' where I've switched to another part of the personality, and the integrating strands of memory haven't carried through to my main stream of consciousness. I feel depersonalised and derealised. I smell memories—odours not from the here-and-now, but from the there-and-then. I experience 'body memories'. I feel myself slipping into a deep well within myself, and the voice that emanates from my mouth sounds child-like and confused. I observe my surroundings as through a tunnel, detached and out-of-control. This is the reality of my subjective experience of DID. It's not hard to see how our 'symptoms'—these experiences born of the disintegrating effects of trauma—dominate our vision, our hearing, our thoughts, our sense of self, our volition. Knowing that we are different, we seek out others who share our 'sanity'. It's a relief to find others who experience life like we do. It's a relief to know that we are not alone, and maybe not so crazy after all.

But recovery insists that we keep our sights set also on the beyond, not just on the now. Our symptoms are real and valid and true. But there is also a beyond, and recovery insists, even in the chaos and turbulence and stupor of dissociation, that we retain the knowledge that our symptoms are the symptoms of trauma, and trauma can be healed. It doesn't feel like it, when the entirety of our self is consumed in the shudder of a frightened four-year-old part of us. It doesn't feel like it when the pain and distress is intolerable. But recovery means that even in the midst of our misery we begin to 'mentalise'—to step back from our here-and-now, this-is-it experience, and see that there is a wider perspective and that what we are feeling now, we will not always feel, and that other states of mind exist, which we will experience at other times and on other days.

We have to believe that we are more than the sum of our symptoms. When we settle for anything less, we limit our recovery, because we allow ourselves to be defined by what happened to us: the oversensitisation of our neurobiology and the fragmentation of our sense of self. Recovery means that we connect the dots between all the different parts of ourselves: the different experiences, emotions, outlooks; the desires, and hopes and fears; and we become the person that we truly are, the whole that is greater than the sum of all its parts. I had to believe that I was more than a collection of symptoms, and forge forwards into the entirety of my being.

8. Fighting battles we cannot win

For so long, life with DID felt like a battle that I could never win. It was a daily onslaught by a sly, invisible enemy. At first I underestimated how much effort would be required of me to fight through to a place of healing and recovery. It has taken years, and life continued to happen even while I fought: I got sick, others got sick, I had money troubles, relationship troubles, career (or lack of it) troubles, family troubles. I realised eventually that life will not always give us a break while we fight to recover. I was struggling on so many fronts, and eventually I realised that I could not fight and win every battle that came my way. I had to concentrate my efforts, and learn to walk away.

But I wanted to fight. I wanted to fight for justice, of the 'criminal justice' kind. I wanted to fight for treatment and support, for compensation or an apology. We all have our battles. Others fight for the right treatment for the right length of time from the right people; for understanding from the Benefits Agency; for fair treatment from employers; for compassion from family and friends. They are worthy battles. Of course what happened to us as children was wrong; of course we were let down by non-abusing bystanders; of course society shouldn't have let it happen; of course we deserve fair treatment and long-term support and all of our human rights now. But we can't fight every battle every day. Sometimes we have to prioritise.

And sometimes we feel that our recovery is contingent on others: that we will recover if our abusers go to jail; or if we get the 'right' therapist (usually an NHS one); or if we are awarded Disability Living Allowance. Some of these battles are worth fighting, because they are taking ground en route to overall victory. But sometimes we are so caught up in the need to fight—the trauma response of fight, flight and freeze—that we don't stop to think about whom we're fighting, and why, and what the outcome might be. Sometimes the only person we hurt with our fighting is ourselves. What Judith Lewis Herman referred to as a 'survivor mission' is undoubtedly a major part of recovery, but sometimes we're fighting because we're angry, instead of fighting to recover. If we can focus our energies on recovery, we'll find strength later for other battles.

9. Pursuing avoidance

When I was a child, the only thing I could do—literally the only thing—was to push away the consciousness of what was happening, stuff the feelings down into a chasm of emptiness inside, and avoid, avoid, avoid. It's a good strategy, and it worked. It still works now, and sometimes it's essential: when we're at work, or responding to the demands of everyday life, it's a good thing to avoid the trauma, so that we can go on with living. But avoidance was my only strategy for dealing with the trauma. It didn't occur to me that the trauma could be resolved, not just avoided.

Avoidance comes in many forms, perhaps the most potent of which are intellectualisation and fantasy. With the former, we talk about DID, we read about DID, we research DID, we hypothesise about DID. Anything other than facing the trauma, and working it through. We try to drown out the trauma with a multitude of words. With fantasy, we live in a complex world of 'alters' and 'littles' and 'systems' and 'hosts', elaborating what is undeniably real—the polyfragmentation of DID and complex trauma—until our self-representation becomes in itself a form of avoidance. We have picnics, play games, watch cartoons—but it can become our sole focus and we avoid working through traumatic memory, or building secure attachment, or mentalising, or learning to regulate our emotions.

Younger parts are real: I had many of them. Through them I learned to have feelings, to 'go there' a step at a time with the trauma narrative. Through the detachment of being not-me, I could explore concepts of my self and my family and my upbringing that were otherwise too overwhelming. Each of my parts had a function and a purpose. But each also contained a temptation: to avoid the hard edges of adult life, to avoid—as adult, me-me—the reality of the trauma and the tidal wave of emotions it brought with it. I had to work against avoidance—I still do.

I had to commit myself to doing the work, pulling the pieces together, integrating the dissociated fragments, owning this trauma as *my* trauma, owning these feelings as *my* feelings. I had to learn that these echoes of the trauma would not kill me and that I could face it myself: that I didn't need to switch to another part of my personality at the first whiff of a feeling. I had to ask myself why I couldn't be vulnerable myself, rather than switching to a four-year-old representation of myself to ask for help. When my focus was solely on 'being DID', solely on mapping 'who's who' rather than engaging with these disowned parts of me, then the avoidance was a dead-end and I didn't move forwards.

10. Perpetuating the abuse

I never saw myself as an abuser. It was a horrific thought. I hated everything that had ever been done to me, and never would I want to do that to another human being. And I haven't. Not to other people. Only to myself.

The irony was lost on me for a long time: here I was, paying privately for therapy, committing hours every week to the sessions themselves, the travel, the journalling, the preparation. Because I wanted to recover: recover from abuse. And there I was, abusing myself at every juncture: self-harm, criticalness, perfectionism, neglect. Compassion, let alone self-compassion, was a strange concept for me: I had experienced so little of it that I didn't really know what it was. When I experienced compassion from others, at first I assumed it to be a trick, part of the grooming process. Over time I began to realise that it was genuine. The harder part was to show compassion towards myself. It was so much easier—so much more natural!—just to hate myself. Frustration erupted easily within, at my many failures, my many struggles, my seeming inability to 'snap out of it' and 'get a grip'. It was only through accepting that dissociation was logical and that I had done the best I could do, at the time, to survive, that I began to be able to offer—grudgingly at first—any empathy or grace towards myself.

But it transformed things. It meant that on any given day, I could struggle, I could fail... but I didn't then need to add to the struggle by beating myself up for it too. Sometimes the greater pain is the pain we cause ourselves, with our acerbic tongue, our punitive self-loathing. The names we call ourselves: 'failure', 'loser', 'idiot'. The rage we unleash upon ourselves when we feel feelings of neediness, or weakness, or vulnerability. It's all we used to know: that was the environment we grew up in, where soft words and tender words and kind words were rare. But that's not the environment we have to live in now, and we don't have to play victim to ourselves and our own self-hatred. We can learn to show ourselves understanding and compassion, kindness and patience. It didn't happen overnight. It didn't happen, with me, for several years. But I have become convinced that recovery from abuse only and ever comes through putting a stop to the abuse, and especially the abuse that we direct at ourselves. I'm not pathetic, an idiot, stupid, crap. I am a survivor of awful abuse. I did my best to survive it, and I'm doing my best now to recover from it. I'm doing ok. I am ok: to be able to say that, surely, is one sign of recovery.

CHAPTER EIGHTEEN

It wasn't my fault

The haybarn

The straw is so scratchy but he's given me sweets, special ones from his pocket, and he saved them just for me. We're right at the top of the haystack, hidden from view, and I could dance inside because I feel smart and clever and excited and *liked*. He's my friend. So much bigger than me, but his pockets spill forth forbidden things—a penknife, some string, a scroggy old ticket, and packets of crumpled, perfect, can't-believe-it sweets. I've never seen so many. He puts most of them away, glances up at me, smiles a half-smile, and gives me another. He says we can play a game. The straw is all itchy on my bottom and the wind is chill between my legs, but he's big and strong and he smells of earth and horses and oil. Every time we meet we play this game, hidden up in the bales with just the hens clucking below. Every time the game gets harder. But every time, without fail, he brings sweets. I feel a bit queasy after a while, and I'm jittery on the inside that I won't want my tea. I feel sunken and hollow with the badness of what I've done. *Don't tell anyone*, I want to say, and when I limp back to the farmhouse later, I know that I won't tell anyone either.

The cot

Always the room is dusk-dark. Ornate, mock-gold picture frames with dismal scenes, glaring down at me through grubby old cot bars. A huge cot, big enough to spin around in, one side dropped down so that it's nearly a bed. The lampshade is an old street scene, with windows as holes in the shade. Shire horses and bronze ornaments and a Greek god hunting with a dog. It is fusty, and old, and drab, and unloved. Voices through the paned-glass door: another argument. And then, when it's dark, when there are no more voices and no more light, he appears at the side of the cot. I can smell him before I can see him. He pulls my hair to come near him, his flies unzipped, something in my mouth. Then *Shh!*, the finger to the lips, bending down, close to my ear so that I feel sick at the reek of his breath. *You're a naughty girl*, he says, and the shame flushes hot against my cheeks. *You're a naughty girl*—again and again, until I feel that my skin will burn with the shame of it. Then, cool relief: *It's a good job I won't tell your mother.* Terror now clenching up inside me, pulling my fingernails into my palms, anything but that, anything but anything but anything but that. *I'll do anything*, I think, and I mean it. *Just don't tell <u>her</u>.*

The rubber ring

I'm dancing. Stuffed to the rim with the joy of holidays, I'm a *yippee* away from us getting in the car. All our bags packed, like lumps of happiness, in the lounge with the fire where Santa comes down. Ready for the plane. Ready for the sea. Grandad is smoking in the armchair next to me. Like he always does; like I always wish he didn't. I blow hard and noisily into the ring. I need to check it's not leaking. I'm going to jump in the pool in it, swim in the sea with it; I love it, I love it, it's mine. I blow until there's no breath left in me, and it's taut-tight yellow and blue. I wear it around me, and dance like I'm paddling. I am delirious. The delight of this holiday, the delight of my ring. Then *whoosh*. My glee falls to the floor, deflated, and so am I. And there is grandad, a wicked, taunting, devilish look on his face, and he brushes away the cinders of ash from the hole in my ring. *How could he do that?* But then it's *smack* for being so naughty, as mummy enters the room, *smack* for dancing around so carelessly, for bumping into grandad, *smack* because I could have started a fire, *smack* because I told you just to wait nicely. And quivering I look up at him and beseech with my eyes, but back comes thunder, the look that says, *Don't you dare.* Then all I can feel is the sting of the smacks, the uprush of guilt, of badness, of *look what I've done*, and *it's all my fault* and *how bad am I*. He relights his cigarette, and she disappears through the thwack-smack doors that flap both ways like in a Saturday morning Western. And now there will be no swimming or jumping or splashing or fun, and I've only got myself to blame.

The sugar bowl

It's only a bowl of sugar, I want to say, but the defiance in me withers away in the backdraft of her rage. *I didn't mean to drop it. I was just trying to be helpful.* But now I am sent to my room, and the day stretches ahead of me, Sunday lunchtime all the way through until bedtime, with this pestering, sulphurous fear inside me of how to put it right. I'm not allowed out, so I can't put it right. Slowly the daylight fades and I wonder if I'll be in trouble for putting my light on. I daren't do anything in case it's not allowed. I stretch out on my bed and hold everything tight in, so that it won't get me in trouble and I won't drop anything again. I cleared up the sugar, swept it all up, wiped it all down, and it was just a *tiny bowl*, just enough for grandad's tea. It's not *that* expensive, is it? Could I do some jobs instead? Could I say sorry, and that be enough? But it's not and I lie here all day, not daring to move, with thick dread heavy on my heart. Because when mum is cross, when mum is cross... I can't breathe with the terror of it. There's only one way to appease her, and I don't know when that will be, but I'd do anything now not to drop the sugar. And has she forgotten me? Up here, blanketed in dark, not daring to put the light on. Has she forgotten me? I wish she would! But I am sore with her unforgiveness, swollen to every part of my being. And I am edgy and empty and fragile and fraught, with the fear of what saying sorry will mean. Do I go to bed now? Do I go and say goodnight? All day I've wished the hours away, but now I want sunlight again. My punishment is coming, and I've only got myself to blame.

The fence

I went back to the farmhouse a little while after. First to the outside toilet, across from the kitchen. Trying to rub the red away. But my knickers stayed pink. In my trousers it was dull blotches, could have been anything. But what about those pants? There's a *sob-sob* jerkily rising within because I can't think of a way to get out of this, can't let on what happened, can't be in that much trouble. *You shouldn't eat sweets before mealtimes. You shouldn't climb on the tractor. You shouldn't go into the horses' stalls.* But I've done those things now and I can't make them undone and there's bright scarlet blotches in my knickers, and my fingernails clench up inside my fists again and I want to pass out. *I'll say I fell on a fence,* I think, and relief gushes upwards. There's panic, then cool relief, then panic once more. Everything spurts up inside me and time has gone away and I'm still in the outside loo and someone's going to notice soon. *I fell on the fence when I was climbing over it.* Peering into the future, barely making out the options ahead. *I was going to the other field where the men are.* It feels futile and hopeless. *I fell on the fence.* And I'll get in trouble for it, but not as bad as if she really knew what I did in the stables, and maybe she won't notice the smell of horses, maybe she won't notice the blotches in my jeans. Maybe I should just hide my pants away and 'lose' them. But there's no one home in the farmhouse, and I wait forever for them to come back, dreading it, wanting it, not knowing what to do. I don't mind him hurting me, making it all bleed, as much as I mind getting into trouble with mummy. *I fell on a fence,* I say, and she's full of disgust and despair at this most ridiculous child who can't be trusted just to play nicely, who gets muddy and filthy and shouldn't be climbing at all. But it seems to appease her and I can breathe again, wash it all away in the bath where the foam stings and it hurts like it hurts like it'll never go away. But *I fell on a fence* is enough, and I am safe, I am safe, at least for tonight.

The therapist

She's sitting there, frozen and limp and passive and dead, and then she's red with the rage of it all and then it's too much, too much, and she's flaccid and empty and sallow and lost. In again, out again, over and over until suddenly, unexpectedly, her eyes lift and she looks the stranger in the eye, and out comes this torrid explosion of *It wasn't my fault*. 'No,' says the therapist softly, like she's icing a cake with her words. 'No, it wasn't your fault.' But she's shifting again within herself, and *If it wasn't my fault, then whose was it?* 'Whose was it indeed?' says the stranger, the therapist, and insists with her eyes on an answer. *It wasn't my fault*. But she can't say any more, can't put the blame where it belongs. 7 But something is ripping on the inside, and she can't quite step into the chasm, she can't quite take this furious ball of blame, the attribution of wrongdoing, and take it out of her own lap and put it elsewhere. She's just staring at it, frowning at it, saying, *This doesn't belong to me*, and 'No,' comes the gentle coaxing, 'No, it doesn't belong to you', but it's that agony of the moment of *Then where will it go?* She is stuck in the stickiness of the painfulness of reality. *It wasn't my fault*. 'And it's not your fault now either.' What isn't? Everything. All these symptoms, all this loss, all this madness, all this pain. The night times, the day times, the horror, the fear. 'It's not your fault.' Then *they* did this to me—it's *their* fault? 'What do you think?' Oh, not again, not that question again, not the admission, at last, somehow, somehow… 'What do *you* think?' *It wasn't my fault*. 'No, you're right.' *It was theirs*. 'Yes, yes it was.' And a breath that seemed to come out forever, and tears that started with a pain in the chest, and a pain in the shoulders, and a pain in the throat, until they gush out and fall splash-splash-splash on the space in between them. *It wasn't my fault. It was theirs*. 'Yes.'

CHAPTER NINETEEN

Recovery is my best revenge

I s recovery possible? That's the question that everyone is asking, even when they're not asking it. After a breakdown, perhaps after years in the mental health system, do we have to simply accept that we're broken and that we'll always be broken, or is it possible to live a life where we're back in control again, where we're living as we want to live, where life has purpose and meaning? And what about revenge? What about that indelible desire for retribution and justice that is etched on each of our souls? Does recovery imply that what happened didn't really matter, that our abusers can get away with it scot-free, that we should just 'forgive and forget' and 'move on', as so many people exhort us to do?

When I brought out the first volume of this book last year, I thought long and hard about a title. In the end I settled on *Recovery is my Best Revenge* because implicit within those words are two concepts that I hold very dear. Firstly, the belief that recovery is *possible*—it really is possible—and I know because I have experienced a significant measure of it: I am here, I have survived. Trauma is neither a life sentence nor a death sentence. It can be processed, and we can recover. And the second concept is the self-evident truth that it's not okay that I was abused and traumatised the way I was. Recovery does not make up for what I experienced. It does not erase the past. What happened to me was wrong, and the desire for revenge is, I believe, a wholly righteous one. It's the part of us that stands up in the midst of evil and says, *That ain't right!*

But my revenge has been found *not* in becoming an abuser myself, but in becoming the best human being that I can be: the kind of human being that my abusers definitely were not, and the kind of human being that they didn't want *me* to be either. I want to live as a *human being*, not an *inhuman being*. And I want to live the kind of life that helps *other people* to live as human beings too.

But to live with recovery as your best revenge, you have to believe that there is *hope* for recovery from trauma. If recovery is not possible, then it is so much easier just to slide into the lazy evil of abusing others as your way of coming to terms with what happened to you. But I believe that recovery *is* possible and that we can in fact choose compassion, both for ourselves and others, rather than abuse.

But I do believe that trauma leaves indelible scars, and in order to recover we need to understand what it has done to us. Because trauma is not just a bad thing or even a series of bad things that happened to me in a vacuum, one cloudy day in August 1976. Trauma is something that shaped my brain just as it was developing. It impacted directly on my growing neural circuitry. It made my amygdala, my brain's 'smoke alarm', more sensitive to incoming threat. It limited the connections between my thinking front brain and my survival-based back brain, making me more reactive to that threat. It affected the internal working models I was building of the world I lived in. It destroyed my sense of self, and my sense that I had a right to be alive.

Trauma is not just a 'bad experience' that I haven't been able to get over. Chronic trauma in childhood is a way of life and a way of learning. It defines the way that our brains organise and understand information. Recovery is a slow, hard process, and it cannot be achieved in six sessions or even six months. Because trauma by its very nature is disintegrative, disconnecting and disempowering.

Trauma breaks down the normal integration, the normal joining-up of thoughts, memories, feelings, behaviours, perceptions and sensations. Our memories are disjointed and held as somatosensory fragments. Our feelings don't integrate with our memories. Our thoughts don't integrate with our behaviours. And trauma has a profound effect on our autobiographical sense of self, as we see in my own experience of dissociative identity disorder (DID). I grew up *without* an integrated sense of self: all the different aspects of my experience and my self-identity did not join up together into a coherent whole. So I developed with what is vividly but inaccurately described as 'multiple personalities'. Walt Whitman, the American poet, expressed it well—he said, 'I am large; I contain multitudes.'

Trauma is also disconnecting. At a profound level, trauma impacts our relationships. It teaches us that even the people who should have nurtured us and cared for us—even they can use us and abuse us. The trauma of abuse teaches us that we exist to manage the feelings of others, and that our own feelings must be blocked out of awareness to cope with that. It teaches us that to go on living with 'good mummy' who irons our clothes for school, we must shut out the consciousness of 'bad mummy'. So we grow up with a very one-sided view of people, as *either* angel *or* demon, as *either* good *or* bad, but not as a complex mix of both. We carry a profound mistrust of people into relationships for the rest of our lives: the expectation that what you see is not what you get: the expectation that someone's comfort, or affection, or praise, is a prelude to abuse. And so in our therapeutic relationships, your smile or greeting, or expression of delight, feels like a form of grooming—it feels like the prelude to abuse, and we square up to you with fight, or run from you with flight, because unwittingly you have triggered deep within us a vision of our abuser.

Trauma disconnects us not only from other people but also from ourselves, and these are the conflicts that can tear us apart on the inside—in my case, with DID, where the parts of my personality are pitched against each other: the parts of me that want to carry on with daily life and are apparently normal, who cope with the trauma by avoiding it and denying that it ever really happened, and the traumatised, emotional parts of my self who are stuck *in* the trauma, raw as a knife edge, because the trauma has never been brought into consciousness and processed and experienced as being *over*.

Trauma is also profoundly disempowering. I believe that the very essence of trauma is powerlessness. It is that unavoidable, inescapable overwhelm of suffering that we can do nothing about. Some of us learn that it's best never to struggle, to just accept the freeze response and lie still until the danger passes. Perhaps by freezing, perhaps by submitting, it will be over with more quickly and we will be hurt less in the process. *Lie still under the danger passes...* But then, in our minds, the danger never passes, and so we live our lives inhibited by an eternal learned helplessness. We feel inept and incapable and stupid and weak, because when it really mattered, when our lives were at risk, we couldn't even move a muscle. So we feel terribly disempowered by that, as if it means that in the rest of life we will be incapable too. And we think: 'What's the point?! What's the point in trying to recover when I'm too helpless and powerless and stupid and weak to be able to do it?'

Breaking out of that mindset has been my journey over the last decade. I have had to work hard at breaking out of that learned powerlessness. I have had to work hard at overcoming my fundamental mistrust of other people. I have had to work hard at learning to live in a joined-up way where I'm in touch with all of me: where I can stretch backwards to the *me-that-was*, whilst also stretching forwards into the *me-that-can-be*. That's been a battle—a deep, deep struggle. But I can say with all honesty that there is a point to it all, because there *is* recovery from trauma and I'm living it. I'm doing things now that I never thought would be possible, even just a few years ago.

But—and there is a big 'but'—for there to be recovery, we need other people. It was 'other people' who caused the damage in the first place, and I believe that we need *other* 'other people' to help repair it now. And that's where therapists come in. Because therapy can help to provide the 'someone' that is needed to move a trauma survivor like me along in life, out of the realm of flashbacks and body memories and nightmares and freeze, and into a place where we can both *think and feel*: a place where we are not just plagued with intrusive thoughts and images and memories that we cannot face alone, but where we can start to mentalise and think *about* the trauma rather than just reliving it. Therapy can provide the place for us to begin to feel the feelings that were frozen at the time, rather than those feelings coming out in somatic symptoms alone. Because one of the unacknowledged realities of trauma is that it carries with it a devastating retinue of physical impacts, everything from heart disease to cancer, to diabetes to rheumatoid arthritis, to ME and fibromyalgia. This is one of my biggest areas of ongoing struggle. In my life, physical ill health has been as much a problem as mental ill health has been. But it's an area, again, where therapy has made a difference more than drugs have. Because so much physical ill health has its seeds in the trauma that we suffered as children, and as I've faced that and dealt with it, so my physical health has improved as well. There is no mindbody split— that's a false dichotomy, and in reality we live as integrated wholes, whatever Descartes had to say about it.

I've had in therapy a 'safe enough' place, a 'secure enough base' to begin to explore who I *really* am. Trauma told me that I am a victim, but through therapy I've become to see myself as a resilient survivor. I survived horror *without support* as a child. And now as an adult I can transform that suffering into compassion both for myself and for others.

Therapy has been life-changing for me. But when I walked into my therapist's office in May 2006, she was just a trainee with very little experience of *counselling* let alone dissociative disorders and organised and extreme abuse. If we go by some of the textbooks, she shouldn't even have started seeing me. Of course I didn't present in that first session with 'multiple personalities'. I did my best to 'act normal' so that I didn't drive her away, because after a year of floundering around in the midst of a breakdown that hit me out of nowhere, towards the end of that first session, she looked me in the eye and said with a fierce but kindly determination, 'I can help you'.

Those four words transformed my life. Because for the first time, I'd found someone who didn't run away from me, who didn't disbelieve me, who didn't tell me that I just needed to pull myself together. She said, 'I can help you'. And she was just a normal human being, without much training, without much experience. And yet she has had a significant impact on my life.

For many of us, the experience of trauma has been such a *lonely* one, so isolating, that the biggest shift for us is when someone is just present, and promises to remain present, while we work things through. The presence of another human being is transformative. This therapist has listened to me, and heard me speak of things that I thought were unspeakable. And through that, she has helped me to realise that I am *just* a human being, just like her. I am not a label, I am not a mental health patient, I am not a victim. I am just a human being, just like her, but one who has had some extreme experiences of suffering which have not yet had the opportunity to heal.

And it can be easy to talk about 'suffering' and 'trauma' as if it's some ethereal, nebulous pseudo-event. But really we're talking about real things happening to real people. I tried to dissociate from the trauma I experienced, to say that it didn't happen, and it didn't happen to *me*. But it did, and recovery has come through accepting those experiences as my own, rather than pushing them away.

Of course this therapist didn't have much experience of dissociative disorders and ritualised and organised abuse. But in many ways, all the reasons why she *shouldn't* have started work with me are the reasons why she's been *so successful* in working with me—because she's been humble, and open, and curious, and willing to learn: all the things I've needed to be to rediscover who I am, too, and heal from this suffering. She wasn't such an 'expert' that she could afford not to listen to me. She wasn't such an 'expert' that she tried to do anything more at first than just be a safe person, a witness, a reassuring presence. She was open-minded, and despite her lack of direct experience, she was actually incredibly wise. And she had a great deal of integrity— she was solid, and grounded, and right from the start, she treated me with a dignity and a respect that had been rare in my life.

I was manifesting very strange behaviours, but she didn't treat me as if *I* were strange. And yet of course it *is* very strange when someone switches to another part of their personality for the first time, when they start talking with a completely different tone of voice, with different facial expressions and a different way of holding their body. But she saw through my symptoms and my behaviours and she saw me as a person. And in over 8 years now, she has never for one moment treated me as anything less than an equal human being who deserves to be listened to and respected.

What she seemed to instinctively grasp was that all my symptoms, and all my behaviours, were *communications*. They were me trying to tell my story, trying to speak when I had been forbidden ever to tell. They were my dissociative unconscious desperately forcing itself into consciousness. They weren't a sign of my madness—they were a sign of my sanity, because my mind wanted to heal. She understood, and I began to understand, that DID is a sane response to some very insane things that happened to me in childhood. After all, how is a child to survive those kinds of experiences, except by chopping them up into more manageable little chunks, and hiding them away in boxes in our mind that we try never to open? What better way to cope with uncopeable realities than by saying that they're not real, by saying that they didn't happen—or at the very least that they didn't happen to *me*? And she has coaxed that communication out of me, and given me a place to speak.

Many, many other people in my life ran away from me during this time. I think, deep down, they were afraid of my suffering, and they didn't know how to handle it. I'm so grateful that my therapist didn't run away. She has never rescued me, and nor has she ever abandoned me. At times, the pressure to run was huge. She was hearing me not just retell but many times *relive* some of the most horrendous, atrocious forms of abuse. When I have been unable to face my trauma, and I've escaped in my head and I've dissociated, she's had to face it down all by herself. She hasn't had the luxury of dissociation. She hasn't had the luxury of overdosing or getting drunk or self-harm or overwork. She's just had to be able to sit with the unbearable suffering of another human being and *feel it*—every last ounce of unbearability and pain. She's had to draw on all her own internal grounding strategies, her self-soothing strategies, her mentalising capacity, to be able to deal with what she's heard. She's had to hold onto her faith in the universe and her faith in humanity and her faith in the process of therapy that this stuff can heal.

And by doing so, she has shown me that there is another way to deal with trauma other than by dissociating from it. She has shown me that there *are* things that we can do to manage our emotions when they threaten to overwhelm us: there is breathing and mindfulness, there is nature and birdwatching and sunsets and stargazing, there is comedy and friendship and holidays and sleep. She has shown me that I can stand back from what happened to me, rather than being sucked into endlessly reexperiencing it. She has shown me that I can hold it in my mind as an event that happened to me, that I can think about it and I can feel the feelings I have about it. I can hold it in mind rather than pushing it out of mind with dissociation. She has shown me that I can feel its feelings rather than avoiding them through numbing or minimising or self-medication or self-harm.

She taught me that feelings are meant to be felt and thoughts are meant to be thought and that dissociation doesn't achieve either. She has shown me that if I can both think and feel at the same time, then my hippocampus—my memory system's 'context stamp'—can tag the memory as 'over', that it *has happened*, that it's in the past. She has shown me that it's okay to have feelings—even strong feelings— about the things that happened to me. She has shown me that it's okay for me to express those feelings, and that I can choose good ways, rather than destructive ways, to express those feelings.

And she has done all of these things, not through some application of heavy textbook theory and a thousand CPD hours, but through the quality of who she is as a human being. Of course I believe that textbooks and theory are important, and that CPD is important—after all I spend a lot of my time delivering CPD and studying textbooks! But I believe the fundamental difference that therapists can make to people like me is in *who you intrinsically are*. It's your character, ultimately, that counts. The theory, the textbooks, the CPD—they are incredibly useful tools. But it's you as a person that counts, and therefore how you use those tools. I believe that 'good enough' therapy requires a 'good enough' therapist who is a 'good enough' human being.

Are therapists peddling a technique? Or are they fundamentally restoring someone's sense of dignity and respect as a valuable and precious human being? Suzette Boon says:

> The therapeutic relationship is the most important vehicle in the treatment of patients with complex dissociative disorders. Patients heal from their early interpersonal trauma in a safe therapeutic relationship that respects healthy boundaries.

The good news there is that patients—clients—do *heal*. And we achieve that through at least three things. Firstly, you can help our brains to see that the trauma is over. It won't work if *you* don't believe that this is so. If you can't see that the trauma is something that *happened to us* but that it is *not us*; if you are intimidated or entranced by our labels, and you forget that we are *just* a traumatised human being—no more, no less—then you won't help us see that trauma is something that happened to us, but that it doesn't need to define us. What we're experiencing is *just* a flashback, it's *just* a feeling, it's *just* a body memory. Don't let trauma intimidate you. The trauma is past; we just need our brains to realise it. So the first step is that your brains realise it too.

Secondly, you can help us to develop 'earned secure' attachment. We have missed out on the ability to mentalise, to think about our thoughts, to stand back from ourselves and our experience and notice it rather than being *in it*. Peter Fonagy says that mentalising is being able to see ourselves from the outside and other people from the inside. Many of us as trauma survivors struggle to do that, because there was never an 'other' to see from the inside; there was never an 'other' who could help us to see ourselves from another perspective. Therapy provides that opportunity—to think about our thoughts, and to begin to see the filter through which we see the world and ourselves—what Bowlby termed our 'internal working model'.

And we have also missed out on the ability to 'affect regulate', to manage our emotions and feelings. Dissociation is what you do when you don't have any other affect regulating mechanism to deal with this overwhelm of feelings from trauma, but then dissociation becomes the only tool we have to manage our feelings, so we need to build up other means of regulating our emotions. This happens, as Allan Schore puts it, in right brain to right brain attunement. It's bad enough that we have experienced such awful suffering in the first place, but that suffering is compounded by our inability to be soothed in our distress. When we feel that there is no soothing, then we will continue to dissociate and the trauma will never be processed and healed. But if we can learn to manage our distress, if we can 'regulate' our 'affect', if we can learn to receive comfort from others and to self-soothe in ways that do not block out the pain, if we can learn to sit with the pain until it passes... then we *can* overcome our suffering.

And thirdly, you can help us to make meaning of our lives and our experiences that is '*post*-post-traumatic'. Living in a post-traumatic worldview, we believe that everything is dangerous and that we have no tomorrow. But it's not enough to try to develop a sanitised worldview, one that pretends that the trauma wasn't there or that it didn't happen. I live with the reality of my scars, without a family, whether I like it or not. Much better is to develop a post-post-traumatic worldview—one that can integrate the safe and the unsafe and say: 'Bad things happened, but I also overcame them and if they happen again, I can overcome them again.'

I have had to change my view of myself: from someone who was chronically overwhelmed and disempowered, to someone who survived—a survivor in the very best sense of the word. I went through the worst, as a child, on my own: I survived *that*. So I can surely survive *this*, now, as an adult, with support. I am resilient—because I didn't give up, I haven't given up, I keep going. The post-post traumatic worldview accepts the reality of what happened, but it also accepts the reality that we survived what happened, that we are amazing, that our lives have value, and that we are precious, resourceful, courageous human beings.

Bad stuff happens and it can drive us crazy. But we can also survive the bad stuff, and we can overcome its scars. We are not 'mad people' with labels, we are just traumatised human beings. You as therapists don't need to be experts. You need to be compassionate human beings who are safe, and who will treat us with dignity and respect as equal human beings who are able to recover from our experiences, because we have already survived them. You just need to come alongside us. You need to provide good enough therapy as good enough therapists who are good enough human beings. You need to be able to sit with us in our unbearable suffering and neither rescue us nor abandon us. You need to be able to step back from our trauma and recognise that it is *our* trauma, not yours, and that it *has happened* but that it is *no longer happening*. You need to see our trauma as something that happened to us, not as something that defines who we are. And you need to believe that there is recovery from trauma, because there really *really* is: recovery *can be* our best revenge.

CHAPTER TWENTY

This is my new life

The sand stretches away into the blue fuzz of horizon. It's white and pure and perfect and still, with whirls of wind painted in it. The water is icy and clear. Along the beach we walk, along and along, walking and walking in this sumptuous, beautiful place. The dog is barking for seaweed. There is no one else anywhere around. The sand is so fine, and the water so clear, and I've never seen anything like it before. *Bark, bark, bark* to throw the ball. *Bark, bark, bark* to fetch it. Little bobbles of cloud in a deep blue sky. Foamy waves licking at my soles. It's all so clean. It's all so fresh. It's all so new. I can't quite believe I'm here. There is no abuse here. Nothing bad, nothing unclean. There is no pain here. There is just goodness and cleanness and fullness of joy. I've never seen anything quite like it. *Bark, bark, bark* at some flotsam. The sun is warm and the air is cold and everything makes me shiver with wonder. This is a new kind of place, a new kind of experience. I can't quite believe it.

I don't mind, I want to say, but for the first time I think I do. From instinct I begin to shrug my shoulders, but deep down somewhere on the inside there's a stirring and I know that really I want to say yes. *Is it allowed?* I want to ask, because this would be two good things in one day, and all of me is unsure. I'd love an ice cream, but I'm an adult now, and I don't know if this is ok. We've walked along the beach and we've picnicked on the headland. We've breathed in goodness, and everything is fizzing with happiness on the inside, and I don't know if I'm allowed to have that feeling, don't know if I'm allowed to keep it. *Do I want an ice cream?* Yes I do. I know I do. Too many good things? What will happen if I have it? What will happen if I want it? Bad things, horrible things, painful things, unspeakable things? No, this is a new life where those things don't happen. I can have an ice cream now, and I won't be hurt later. It's just an ice cream, just a good thing, and it's ok for me to have it. There's a shudder inside, like the burp of some dread, but I just nod at myself quietly. *It's ok,* I say, and I mean it. *It's ok to have good things,* and I know that that's true. It's taken a lot of shifting, to believe that, and instinct still pulls me to shake my head. But this is my new life, this is a good life, and we eat ice creams as we drive near cliffs rimmed by rainbows. I do mind, and it's good.

At first they were just specks in the sky, three specks circling, up high on the wind drift, up high above the world. We stopped the car and got out. Binoculars. *It might be...* It's probably not... *It is, you know, it is.* I look for the markings, for the wingspan, for the flight. The tails splays out like a fan. It's soaring and gliding, holding its wings in a shallow 'V'. It's drawing a circle in the sky. Next to it, on its inside, are two smaller ones, its young. At the end of its wings, huge and broad and majestic and golden, it reaches out its fingers. I can just make out the inner feathers, white like snow. *It is, you know, it is.* Excitement rises like a gulp in my throat. *You might be right.* And I am. A golden eagle, with two of its young, fainting against the sky on this most beautiful of days. All my life I had wanted to see one. I used to dream about it, write about it, talk to anyone who would listen. *A golden eagle.* I can't quite believe it. And not one but three. *Is it allowed?* Yes, it's allowed. This is our new life, where good things are allowed.

It's a funny little boat, a bit like the Lego one I had as a child, but all around us is the deep smoky blue of the Kyle flowing out into the North Sea and it is wonderful and desolate and I'm humming on the inside with the sheer pleasure of being here. We bounce off the tops of the waves, spray shimmering up behind us. I've never been out on a boat quite like this before. I've never fished. We sit in the lapping silence, the beauty of the sky and the sunlight jagged on the water, and for the first time I feel at home within myself. *Is it allowed?* I wonder, almost out loud. *Yes, yes, it's allowed,* I reassure myself and I am nearly breathless with the joy that it is. We poke our rods out the back of the boat, waiting, barely daring to hope, but one little mackerel after another tugs at the line and then squirms around in our bucket, our evening meal. The wind is mild and invigorating. There's no badness here, no evil, no pain. This is a world away from what I thought was normal. I can't quite believe that it's real. The joy on the inside of me sits on a deep layer of sadness that I feel on every wave roll. I realise how wrong the badness was. I realise how much goodness there can be, and I'm sad and angry that I didn't know it until now. And then I breathe again, let my eyes wander around the cliffs of the island we are now picnicking by, and the joy swells harder. *This is what life can be like now,* I say to myself, and I want to cry because I know it's true.

For part of the morning we wander around the beach, clamber up into rockpools, *bark bark* goes the dog to chase a stone, and I'm fascinated by the stripes of ochre and grey in the cliffstones around us. We drive out onto the headland, and scramble over dunes. We drive into the wilderness, and Ben This and Ben Something Else crowd the sky around us. *This is my new life, where good things are allowed,* I say to myself, to try to make myself believe it. The landscape is so expansive, like it's opening wide its arms and filling deep its lungs, and all this crisp, earthy goodness makes me want to sing. *Good things are allowed,* I say again, and I'm aware of them for the first time. I want to sow them. I want to cultivate them. I want to grow them like seedlings. It's not enough to dredge away the bad stuff. I've got to grow the good stuff too. I've got to learn how to live. And here, in this place, like no place I've ever been before, it feels right to have good things. It feels right to be alive. It feels like something has shifted. It's no longer just about surviving the bad stuff. It's about living the good stuff too. And I want to, and that feels ok, and new life shivers deliciously up my spine and I want to shout to my abusers, tell them that they haven't won, that I'm here and it's wonderful, and they can't stop me coming back. I feel strong and tall and powerful and alive. *This is my new life,* I say again, and everyone on the inside agrees, *where good things are allowed.*